LIVING CHRIST

PAUL'S ADVICE FOR EVERYDAY LIFE

LIVING CHRIST

PAUL'S ADVICE FOR EVERYDAY LIFE

EVERETT LEADINGHAM, editor

Though this book is designed for group study,
it is also intended for personal enjoyment and
spiritual growth. A leader's guide is available
from your local bookstore or your publisher.

BEACON HILL PRESS
OF KANSAS CITY

Editor
Everett Leadingham
Managing Editor
Charlie L. Yourdon
Senior Executive Editor
Merritt J. Nielson

Copyright 2006
Beacon Hill Press of Kansas City
Kansas City, Missouri

ISBN: 083-412-1905
Printed in the United States of America

Cover Design
Chad A. Cherry
Interior Design
Sharon Page

10 9 8 7 6 5 4 3 2 1

CONTENTS

WHY CHANGE?

BY GEORGE LYONS

From: DISCIPLE@21STCENTURY.CHURCH

To: PAUL@APOSTLES.CHRIST

Subject: Conversion

Dear Brother Paul,

We don't get it. We thought you told us that God loved us just as we were—Gentile sinners. So why are you so insistent that we totally change? Our neighbors already think we're weird for what we've done—listening to a Jewish itinerant preacher and gathering together to sing and share communal meals on Sundays. Some believers here are thinking about getting circumcised just like you Jews. Is this the kind of change you're after? Others say that it really doesn't matter what we do or don't do, reminding us of what you said about God's grace being greater than our sins. Please, explain your position. What changes did you make when you became a Christian?

A Concerned Believer

Reading someone else's mail is a bit like overhearing one side of a telephone conversation. We hear only enough to become curious. If this half of the conversation is especially juicy, we may be sorely tempted to sneak to an extension phone and eavesdrop quietly. (But you've never done that, right?)

It is clear from what we read in Paul's letters that we have only part of an ongoing conversation. Nearly 2,000 years removed, we wish in vain for an opportunity to "hear" what was being said on the other end of the line.

We can only speculate about what Paul's first readers asked him. However, knowing a bit more about how people lived and thought in the first-century eastern Mediterranean world significantly improves our educated guesses.

DIFFERENT ASSUMPTIONS

When we read Paul's letters with modern Western "spectacles," we often assume that Paul was answering different questions than his original audience could possibly have asked.

Modern psychology has profoundly influenced the way we think about people and cultures. We assume that childhood influences and experiences significantly shape our lives, that we inevitably change and develop over time, and that change is good. Yet, that is not how ancient Mediterranean people thought at all. Familiarity with ancient "biographies" will help free us of such modern notions. (If you don't believe me, search the Internet and read some of Plutarch's *Lives.*) These are not the kind of biographies we expect—chronologically sequenced, womb-to-tomb analyses of (say) how an obscure child of uneducated social misfits, born in a log cabin, eventually became the man who would occupy the White House. Instead, ancient biographies relate disconnected anecdotes, vignettes that reveal a person's unwavering character.

In antiquity, people did not assume our current theories of personality development. Rather, it was believed that gender, generation, and geography determine a person's identity, which is to say it is fixed at birth. Paul or anyone else who claimed to have become a different person as a result of some experience (such as conversion) would likely be seen as a deviant, liar, or outcast.[1]

WHAT'S YOUR NAME?

In the absence of the surnames we take for granted, ancient people were identified by patronomics—their father's names. For example, among the twelve apostles were "James son of Zebedee" and "James son of Alphaeus" (Matthew 10:2-3). Sons normally pursued their father's trade. James and John were fishermen like their father, Zebedee (see 4:21-22). People still say, "Like father, like son."

Jesus, adoptive son of Joseph the carpenter, was naturally a carpenter himself (see Mark 6:3). That is, until He attended a "revival meeting" conducted by John the son of Zechariah in the Jordan River. When John reluctantly baptized Jesus, a heavenly vocation forever changed His life's direction (see Matthew 3:13-17). Thus, He became known as, "Jesus, the prophet from Nazareth in Galilee" (Matthew 21:11) and "the Teacher" (26:18). Still, His calling made Him suspect to those who knew Him best. "Only in his hometown, among his relatives and in his own house is a prophet without honor" (Mark 6:4).

The Nazarenes who called Jesus "Mary's son" (6:3) probably intended to challenge the legitimacy of His birth. His dramatic life-change that overturned cultural norms even led some to conclude, "He has a demon," and to malign Him as "a glutton and a drunkard" (Matthew 11:18-19; Luke 7:33-34). Their insult reflected the provisions of Deuteronomy 21:18-21, calling for the death by stoning of "a stubborn and rebellious son," who refused to fit in. Jesus' scandalous associations—"a friend of tax collectors and 'sinners'" (Matthew 11:19; Luke 7:34) and His prophetic vocation made Him a social and religious outcast. When the Jewish religious establishment finally had Him crucified because they thought He was a messianic pretender, His followers shared His stigma.

We would hesitate to label the change that occurred in Jesus' life when He was about 30 a "conversion." There is no reason to believe He had been a sinner needing to repent. Nevertheless, Jesus' change made it possible for us, who were such sinners, to come to God. We all had the wrong father, hailed from the wrong place, and belonged to the wrong crowd.

WHERE ARE YOU FROM?

Not only genealogy, but geography was an important source of personal identity in antiquity. Peter's distinctive Galilean accent (see Matthew 26:73) led some to dismiss him as an uneducated, country hick (see Acts 4:13). Nathanael hesitated to accept Philip's claim that Jesus was the Messiah simply because of His hometown. "Nazareth! Can anything good come from there?" (John 1:46). Who today is so closely identified with his or her hometown as "Jesus of Nazareth" (as He is identified throughout the Gospels and Acts) or Saul of Tarsus (see Acts 9:11; 21:39; 22:3)?

Tarsus, unlike Nazareth, had a sterling reputation as one of the leading university towns of the Roman Empire. Yet from the Jewish perspective, this did not compensate for its location as the residence of scattered Jews. Expatriate Jews from far-flung Gentile territories outside Jerusalem and Judea had to prove themselves trustworthy. This may explain Saul's excessive zeal for his ancestral traditions (see Galatians 1:14).

ONE OF US OR ONE OF THEM?

Although nation-states in the modern sense did not exist in antiquity, ethnic stereotypes and racial prejudices were rife.

Greek-speakers regarded everyone else as barbarians. Jews similarly divided the world into two groups: those who were not "Jews by birth" were "Gentile sinners" (Galatians 2:15).

John the Baptist had warned the religious establishment, "Do not think you can say to yourselves, 'We have Abraham as our father.' I tell you that out of these stones God can raise up children for Abraham" (Matthew 3:9; Luke 3:8). Jesus similarly dismissed the usual assumptions associated with Jewish particularity (see John 8:31-47).

Jesus' fellow Nazarenes were favorably impressed by the program of His inaugural sermon in His hometown synagogue. That is, until He reminded them that the long-awaited year of Jubilee, with its good news for the poor, liberation for prisoners, and sight for the blind, was to include Gentiles. Then they drove Him out of town and tried to stone Him to death (see Luke 4:14-30).

DON'T ROCK THE BOAT!

This was the last straw in Jesus' unremitting challenge to His contemporaries' cultural and religious stereotypes and stigmas about gender, genealogy, and geography. This undoubtedly contributed to their decision to crucify Him as a danger to the status quo. And it also explains why a zealous Jew like Saul of Tarsus, anxious to demonstrate his loyalty to Judaism, would throw himself into the cause of persecuting the followers of the crucified Nazarene (see Galatians 1:13-14; Acts 7:54—8:1).

Jesus' conviction that the kingdom of God was open to all who would repent threatened to tear down the wall separating Jews and non-Jews. It suggested that Jews and Gentiles alike were sinners; that Gentiles need not follow Jewish customs to enjoy a right relationship with God; that people were not justified by observing the Law, but by the faithfulness of Jesus the Messiah—a faithfulness that resulted in His crucifixion (see Galatians 2:14-21).

FROM PERSECUTOR TO PREACHER

Saul of Tarsus persecuted Christians precisely because
he saw the Cross as proof that Jesus was under the curse of
God (see Galatians 3:13). But when he met the risen Lord
on the Damascus road, the persecutor became a preacher of
the faith he had previously tried to destroy (see 1:23). He
saw the Cross in an entirely new light. "I will boast only
about the cross of our Lord Jesus Christ; for by means of his
cross the world is dead to me, and I am dead to the world"
(Galatians 6:14, TEV). The Cross was not merely the instrument of death upon which Jesus died. It became the focal
point of His mission (see 6:17).

Saul's conversion did not cause him to change his mind
about the implications of the life and ministry of Jesus. He
merely changed sides, because he could no longer regard
Christ from "a worldly point of view" (2 Corinthians 5:16).
It was not a guilty conscience over the stoning of Stephen
that drove Saul to his knees on the Damascus road. It was
the unexpected revelation that Jesus of Nazareth was the
risen Messiah His followers claimed Him to be.

Even Christians at first had difficulty accepting the
news of Saul's conversion. Nevertheless, the evidence of his
changed allegiance that persuaded them to accept him also
led his former associates to begin to persecute him (see
Galatians 1:23-24; 5:11).

CONVERSION OR CALL?

Saul's "conversion" was not the result of a guilty conscience or the study of theology. It came as a powerful revelation from God of the reality of the resurrected Jesus. Saul
did not change gods or religions. He continued to worship
the God of Israel and to be a Jew, but his understanding of
both was dramatically altered. Such a radical change in
worldview can properly be called a conversion.

Still, Saul's was not a "conversion" in the way we normally think of one. It was certainly not the kind of conversion he expected of his Gentile converts. Paul had never been guilty of idolatry or the gross sins that had characterized the lives of most pagans. In fact, as far as "legalistic righteousness" was concerned, he considered himself "faultless" (Philippians 3:6). Only in light of Christ did he see his pre-Christian life as rubbish (see vv. 7-11).

Saul's "conversion" was a "vocation" to preach Christ to Gentiles (Acts 9:15), who needed to be changed even more urgently than he did. Saul was called to continue and extend the mission of Jesus beyond the comfortable boundaries human culture had erected based on race, ethnicity, gender, geography, and so on. For a self-righteous Pharisee to be able to do this definitely called for a "conversion."

Paul's Jewish detractors maligned his law-free mission to the Gentiles as soft-peddling the truth (see Romans 3:8). However, Paul saw himself as a minister of Christ to the Gentiles in the priestly service of the gospel of God, so that the offering of the Gentiles might be acceptable, sanctified by the Holy Spirit. That is, his work for God was to win obedience from the Gentiles (see Romans 15:16-18). God had set him "apart for the gospel of God" (Romans 1:1), and given him the grace to fulfill his apostolic calling to bring about the obedience of faith among the Gentiles (see v. 5).

DEATH TO THE LAW

None of Paul's letters gives a narrative account of his "conversion" as reported three times in Acts (see chaps. 9, 22, and 26). He never speaks of his outward experience, but only of its theological implications.

> For through the law I died to the law so that I might live for God. I have been crucified with Christ and I no longer live, but Christ lives in me. The life I live in the body, I live by faith in the Son of God, who loved me and gave himself for me (Galatians 2:19-20).

Paul was persuaded that if salvation were possible through law, human status, or achievement, "Christ died for nothing!" (v. 21).

Paul did not oppose the law as the revealed will of God. On the contrary, he insisted that "the law is holy, and the commandment is holy, righteous and good" (Romans 7:12). The status quo, not law, is the real threat. Law is powerless to give life (see Galatians 3:21). It can *diagnose* the human problem; it can even *prescribe* a cure; but it cannot *empower* people to change from rebellion to obedience.

God does not condemn Christians for their former sins, because Christ has set them free from their old lives. God has done what the law was unable to do with weak human beings. By sending his Son in the likeness of sinful humanity, God has instead condemned sin so that those who live in the power of the Spirit, and not their own strength, can actually fulfill what the law requires (see Romans 8:1-5).

If people are ever to please God, they must change. But only divine love can do that! To imagine that we don't need saving or that we can save ourselves is to suggest that Christ died for nothing, that new life in Christ is worthless (see Galatians 5:1-12; 6:11-16).

Paul didn't become a Christian because he had failed at law-keeping, but because his successes were so shallow. His own accomplishments were sewage compared to the surpassing significance of Christ (see Galatians 1:14; Philippians 3:2-17).

Just as death is the prerequisite of resurrection, an end to a concept of salvation based on genealogy, geography, gender, and human achievement is the prerequisite of a right relationship with God. God cannot justify those who insist on justifying themselves (see Luke 18:9-14).

The death of Christ on the Cross as the only means of salvation was for most of those who first heard the message a scandal, a stumbling block, total foolishness. Far from a demonstration of God's power, it seemed the proof of His weakness (see 1 Corinthians 1:18-25). Only resurrection could vindicate all Jesus was, said, did, and died for. By the Resurrection, God said that Jesus, rejected by His contemporaries as an accursed outcast, was right and the guardians of the law were wrong.

PEOPLE CAN CHANGE!

Like Jesus, Saul the convert challenged the status quo. If God can raise the dead, people can change! God alone provides the necessary grace to make change possible. Paul's description of his conversion/call echoes that of Jeremiah, who also was called to the Gentiles (compare Galatians 1:15-16 and Jeremiah 1:5). Paul's U-turn was not unprecedented, nor was it of his own initiative.

Despite the assumptions of many of his contemporaries, Paul's turnaround did not make him an unreliable, waffling, fickle opportunist latching on to the latest fad. God was responsible for the 180-degree change in his life's direction. Paul had not volunteered for combat duty; he was drafted. Paul did not change to gain social acceptance or to clear his conscience. This was no midlife crisis; God had decided that Paul should minister to the Gentiles even before he was born.

Acts does not associate the change from the Hebrew name Saul to the Greek name Paul with his Damascus-road experience. He is first called Paul as he begins his Gentile mission (see Acts 13:9). Perhaps he had carried both names since birth. Perhaps Paul was a nickname—*Paulos* means "small one." Or perhaps the name-change was necessitated by his move into the Greek-speaking world where the term *Saulos* described the walk of a prostitute.[2]

THE BEGINNING OF THE END

That God vindicated Jesus through resurrection marked the beginning of the end—the final age of salvation. Darkness at midday! Earthquakes tearing open rocks and Temple veils and tombs! The Cross marked the end of the world as they knew it. That awful Friday was like the great and terrible Day of the Lord described by Old Testament prophets. Cosmic disaster. Judgment. Darkness and gloom.

The mockers at the Cross demanded the wrong sign—that Jesus should come down from the Cross. They missed the clear signs of divine judgment as God himself took the brunt of His wrath against sin! The Cross marks the end of the old order; the Resurrection, the beginning of the new!

"Therefore, if anyone is in Christ, he is a new creation; the old has gone, the new has come!" (2 Corinthians 5:17). As the vestiges of the old age linger on, the whole creation groans in anticipation of the revealing and glorious freedom of the children of God (see Romans 8:18-25).

SO WHY CHANGE?

Like Paul, we "have died to the law through the body of Christ, so that [we] may belong to another, to him who has been raised from the dead in order that we may bear fruit for God" (Romans 7:4).† The revolutionary changes God set in motion with the death and resurrection of Christ are not just about Him or extraordinary Christians like Paul. His story is also to be our story.

Conversion is not just about getting our sins forgiven and our consciences cleared. Sanctification is not just about a second trip to the altar. God intends to involve us in the revolutionary changes He has planned for this planet. If He is to achieve His purposes for the world, He must have a people who will continue the work of Christ, offering good news to all who will receive it. Of course, we will use words as necessary. But our best witness will continue to be, as it was for Paul, the cruciform shape of our lives, dramatically altered by a new mission—a driving passion that all people may come to a saving knowledge of God.

†Author's translation.

Notes:

1. Ben Witherington III, *The Paul Quest: The Renewed Search for the Jew of Tarsus* (Downers Grove, Ill.: InterVarsity Press, 1998), 18.

2. Witherington, 72.

Scripture Cited: Deuteronomy 21:18-21; Matthew 3:9; 4:21-22; 8:10-12; 10:2-3; 11:18-19; 21:11; 26:18; Mark 3:8; 6:3-4; Luke 7:33-34; John 1:46; Acts 9:15; Romans 1:1, 5; 7:4, 12; 2 Corinthians 5:16-17; Galatians 2:15, 19-21, 6:14, 17; Philippians 3:6-11

About the Author: Dr. Lyons is professor of theology and Christian ministries at Northwest Nazarene University in Nampa, Idaho.

WHAT DID JESUS DO?

BY TOM PHILLIPS

From: DISCIPLE@21STCENTURY.CHURCH

To: PAUL@APOSTLES.CHRIST

Subject: Plan of Salvation

Dear Brother Paul,

I have friends who say that they have a relationship with God, but that they aren't interested in learning about Christ. What do you think? What is Christ's role in our salvation? What difference did Jesus' life, death, and resurrection make? Why is the life of one person who lived and died 2,000 years ago so important?

A Concerned Believer

If the apostle Paul were sent an E-mail like the one above, he would probably respond with the blessing in Ephesians 1:3-14. For the apostle Paul, Christian life was rooted firmly in Christ.

Most of Paul's letters, like our letters today, took a familiar shape. In our day, letters typically begin with the sender's and recipient's addresses, the date, and a salutation.

In Paul's day, Christian letters typically began with the sender's name (for example Ephesians 1:1*a*), the recipient's name (1:1*b*), a peace wish (1:2), and a prayer of thanksgiving or blessing. In Ephesians, Paul's familiar prayer takes the form of a blessing (1:3-14). This blessing reminds readers of the blessings that are theirs in Christ.

WHOSE WE ARE

As a professor, I often have young people come into my office and say something like this: "Dr. Phillips, I'm thinking about taking a few years off school to find myself. I want to find myself before I finish school. Right now, I really don't know who I am." When I hear this sort of story, I usually smile, call the student by name, and suggest that he or she is asking the wrong question. "Who am I?" is not the key question, but rather "Whose am I?"

When students are tempted to go on a quest of self-reflection to "discover their true self," I try to redirect them to reflect upon Christ, not upon themselves. Whether they remain in college or not, these inquisitive young people need to understand that the essential principle of human life is not who we are, but rather who Christ is. The fundamental question of human life is, "To whom do we belong?" As Christians, we belong to Christ.

Paul understood the centrality of Christ. In verses 3 through 14 of chapter 1 alone, Ephesians mentions Christ 11 times. The central premise of these verses is that God "has blessed us in Christ with every spiritual blessing" (v. 3). These spiritual blessings are *chosenness* (v. 4), *adoption* (v. 5), *redemption* and *forgiveness* (v. 7), *revelation* (v. 9), a *plan* (v. 10), an *inheritance* (v. 11), and a *hope* (v. 12). As we examine this prayer, we will consider each of these seven blessings in turn.

CHOSENNESS

God "chose us in [Christ]" (v. 4).
Life in the ancient world, like life in our world, was

competitive. People competed for social advantages, jobs, promotions, raises, and even spouses. They competed for honors, recognition, and success in sports, business, and politics. Sometimes they distinguished themselves and their achievements were recognized. Sometimes they were chosen for honors; sometimes they were not.

The letter to the Ephesians told its ancient readers that in Christ, things were different. Everyone has been chosen. God has chosen everyone because of what Christ has done. The competition was over. Being chosen was not contingent upon one's own achievements, abilities, or hard work. Being chosen depended upon one's relationship to Christ. Ephesians announced an end to the competition to be chosen. Chosenness is a gift from God because of Christ's achievement.

As believers, we never have to sit on the sidelines, hoping to be chosen for the team. Or watch the mailbox, hoping to receive a letter of acceptance. Or even linger by the phone, in anticipation of good news about our future. Ephesians is our letter of acceptance. "Don't sweat it," the letter says, "God has already chosen you in Christ."

ADOPTION

God "destined us for adoption as his children through Jesus Christ" (v. 5, NRSV).

In Paul's day, all children were adopted by their fathers. As harsh as it sounds, children belonged to their mothers by birth, but belonged to their fathers only if their fathers chose to adopt them. Therefore, after a woman gave birth, her husband would decide whether or not to adopt the child. Often times, the mother or other concerned family members would try to persuade the father. If the father decided to adopt the child and allow it to share in his family and estate, the father would offer a sacrifice as a sign of official adoption. However, if the father decided not to adopt, the child would often be left along the side of a road to either starve or be raised by strangers as a slave. Such practice was common and made adoption a particularly powerful image for ancient readers.

Into such a world, Ephesians offered the assurance that believers' adoption by their Heavenly Father has been pre-arranged through Jesus Christ. Jesus Christ has already successfully advocated for our adoption. Believers have been "destined for adoption" and have no reason to worry about whether or not their Heavenly Father will adopt them. The believer's adoption has been secured for all time through Jesus Christ!

REDEMPTION AND FORGIVENESS

"We have redemption through his blood, the forgiveness of sins" (v. 7).

Whereas believers' chosenness and adoption start with the goodness of the Father, this blessing in Christ begins in believers' complete lack of goodness. Only those who have sinned need redemption and forgiveness. Though earthly fathers in the first century adopted children during the innocence of their infancy, the believers' redemption and forgiveness came only after sin had brought an end to innocence. Still, through the self-giving love of Christ, even the guilty are assured of redemption and forgiveness.

Forgiveness and redemption are related but different phenomena. Forgiveness is oriented toward the past; redemption toward the future. Forgiveness cancels the deficits of the past; redemption restores value for the future. Through Christ, believers have both forgiveness (release from the guilt of the past) and redemption (restoration of the opportunity for a new future).

In Christ, believers are both freed from the errors of their past and freed to live out a better future. Through Christ, God forgives the sin, rebellion, and folly of our past and offers the prospect of a brighter future. Through Christ, not only can our past be forgiven, but also our future can be redeemed, restored to the beauty that God intended for it.

REVELATION

God "made known to us his will . . . in Christ" (v. 9).

"How do you know that?" "Who told you that?" Such
questions were as common in the ancient world as they are
today. People wanted to know how Paul knew the will of
God, how Paul was sure what God was up to in the world.
In Ephesians, Paul's readers are reminded that the will of
God is fully known because God has been revealed in
Christ. To learn of Christ was to learn of God.

We also live in a world where people are asking questions about God's will. Skeptics sometimes wonder how
Christians can be so confident that the Church really knows,
and the Bible truly reveals, God's will. In a world with so
many competing religious ideas and systems, even sincere
believers can sometimes wonder about such issues. For the
apostle Paul, God's will could be known because it was revealed in a person, Jesus Christ. In Jesus Christ, every intention of God has been made plain.

If you want to know what God is up to in this world, if
you want to know what it would look like for God's dreams
to come true in this world, just look at Jesus. In Christ, the
will of God—God's desire to save all humanity—is fully revealed. Jesus has shown us the full and loving will of God.
And in doing so, Jesus has shown us God's will for our
lives—to love as Christ loved. That's why Ephesians can ad-
monish readers to "live in love, as Christ loved us" (5:2).

A PLAN

*God has "a plan for the fullness of time, to gather up all
things in [Christ]" (v. 10, NRSV).*

In Paul's first-century world, religion was ubiquitous.
Religious images and inscriptions were everywhere. New
gods and goddesses were constantly being imported into the
Roman Empire from different areas within the vast empire.
Ancient cities often played host to temples from dozens of

gods and goddesses, many of whom competed with each other for loyalty of the citizens. Often, worship of these deities appeared to have little direction or purpose.

Jewish worship offered an alternative to the squabbling over deities of Rome and Greece. For Jews like Paul, Yahweh, the God of Israel, offered a specific plan for history. Israel's God had chosen a people and offered them a distinctive hope and future. However, the problem for many non-Jews was that Israel's hope was too narrowly focused on Israel and Israel's future.

In Ephesians, God's plan was extended beyond Israel. As Ephesians later explains, the "dividing wall" between Jews and Gentiles has been "broken down" (see 2:11-22). In fact, through Christ, God's plan has been extended to include "all things" (1:10). God's plan in Christ extended to everything that had been scarred by sin. History is going somewhere, and the direction of history points toward the good news of Jesus Christ for the entire creation.

As believers, who can be distressed by the prevalence of sin and destruction, we are reminded that God has given this world a direction and has set a course for its future through Jesus Christ. Although death, destruction, and heartache often appear to have the upper hand in the present age, God has a plan to overcome all sin through Christ. History is not pointless, and God's plan of redemption will not fail. As Christians, we shall see the fulfillment of all things in Christ!

INHERITANCE

In Christ, we have also obtained an inheritance" (v. 11, NRSV).

Right after talking about God's plan for the future, Ephesians reminds its readers of what they already have obtained in Christ. The apostle Paul often talked about the glories that await Christian believers at Christ's return, but he never allowed expectation of that future blessing to over-whelm the reality of believers' present blessings.

For Paul, believers had already been granted an inheri-tance: the privilege of being united with Christ. The great heritage of Christian faith was to say with Paul, "It is no longer I who live, but it is Christ who lives in me" (Galatians 2:20, NRSV). The birthright of Christian faith was to be bap-tized into Christ. Through baptism, believers could partici-pate in Christ's death (as they entered the water) and resur-rection (as they emerged from the water). By experiencing this transformation from death to resurrection, believers in-herited a new life in Christ. Through their symbolic death and resurrection, believers could consider themselves "dead to sin but alive to God in Christ Jesus" (Romans 6:11).

HOPE

"We . . . were the first to hope in Christ" (v. 12).

Of all the aspects of Paul's thought, hope is probably the least understood and appreciated. For Paul, hope was the fuel that energized Christian faith. It was not merely about the power of positive thinking or the intrinsic value of an optimistic outlook. Hope was the personal conviction that what God had begun in Christ, God would complete in Christ. It was rooted both in Christians' present experience of the goodness of God in Christ and in Christians' expecta-tion of God's continued goodness through Christ. Hope is the confidence that God will bring God's good work to completion through Jesus Christ.

Believers' faithfulness was enabled by the hope of Christ's return and ultimate triumph over evil. Without this future dimension that hope adds to faith, Christians could be tempted to despair over their seemingly unending strug-gle against evil. However with hope in Christ, believers are assured that evil is a defeated foe and that grace will triumph over hate and bitterness. Hope sustains Christians as they battle "against the cosmic powers of this present darkness, against the spiritual forces of evil in heavenly places" (Ephesians 6:12, NRSV).

For Paul, the power of the future hope was so profound that he could say, "If for this life only we have hoped in Christ, we are of all people most to be pitied" (1 Corinthians 15:19, NRSV). When our faith wanes, it's usually because our hope is low. But the resurrected Christ has blessed us with hope. Based upon what has already happened in our lives, we have hope that God will bring it to completion on the day of Christ.

CONCLUSION

We all get legions of unwanted E-mail every day. If the apostle Paul were alive today, he would probably also get his fair share of unwanted messages; and, like us, he would probably delete many of those messages without answering them. However, if he got a message asking about Christ and Christ's role in our salvation, the apostle undoubtedly would have answered with enthusiasm. Paul would have happily proclaimed that we belong to Christ and that belonging to Christ lies at the heart of the Christian life. Belonging to Christ forgives our past, reforms our present, and transforms our future.

For Paul—and for us—Jesus' life, death, and resurrection make all the difference. Through the life of this remarkable individual, the very Son of God, God has made the fullness of salvation available to everyone and secured our place within the plan and purpose of God for now and for eternity. As the central character in the drama of redemption, Christ embodies the love of God, establishing our identity as the people of God, and grounding our hopes as those who look to Him for salvation.

So if you want to know God, look deeply at Jesus. If you want to experience God, talk to Christ in prayer. If you want to make God's dreams come true, follow the example of Christ. If you want to belong to God, give yourself to Christ. As ironic as it may sound, if you want to "find yourself," you must lose your life—and then find it again in Jesus Christ. Life really begins with the simple truth that we belong to Christ, and it is through Christ that all the blessings of God are made known.

Scripture Cited: Romans 6:11; 1 Corinthians 15:19; Galatians 2:20; Ephesians 1:1-14; 2:11-22; 5:2; 6:12

About the Author: Dr. Phillips is assistant professor of New Testament at Colorado Christian University.

CHURCH? WHY BOTHER?

BY C. S. COWLES

From: DISCIPLE@21STCENTURY.CHURCH

To: PAUL@APOSTLES.CHRIST

Subject: Belonging

Dear Brother Paul,

Greetings in the majestic name of Jesus! I am the senior pastor of a rapidly growing church in a cosmopolitan city. My congregation mostly comprises new converts who come from a variety of racial, social, and spiritual backgrounds. Many of these gifted, energetic, and enthusiastic young believers, however, are erratic in church attendance, and reluctant to get involved. How do I cultivate commitment to our local church and loyalty to our denomination's theological tradition?

A Concerned Believer

Roger (not his real name) has been a friend since boyhood days. We found ourselves once again, as young adults, attending the same church, where he found special joy in being a "bus pastor" to unchurched kids. After a series of crushing blows, however, including the loss of his business and his wife, he dropped out of the church.

In later life, he came back to the Lord, and became an enthusiastic participant in Promise Keepers rallies. Attending a rally with 700,000 men was the highpoint of his spiritual renewal. Yet, having once been "burnt" by the church, he shied away from any involvement beyond Sunday morning worship, and his current job as a long-haul trucker has broken even that fragile link. That doesn't seem to bother him, however. He has his Bible, his gospel radio programs, and an occasional truck-stop chapel service. And that is all the church he feels he needs.

Roger is not alone. Thirty-five percent of the unchurched in America—some 23 million people according to the Barna research group—claim to have a personal relationship to Christ quite apart from ongoing participation in a local church. He is typical of our rootless generation where loyalty to a corporate entity of any kind is mostly a thing of the past.

There are striking similarities between the go-it-alone individualism of so many believers today, and that of the Corinthians to whom Paul wrote his most extensive letters. Hopefully, by assessing their cosmopolitan culture and noting how Paul dealt with them, we can tap into some practical New Testament principles that will help us build strong, united, and productive communities of faith.

SALVATION AND CHURCH: THE GREAT DIVORCE

We get acquainted with new people by asking questions about their family, employment, and background. Likewise to understand a church, we must look at its unique historical heritage, geographical setting, and cultural context. What goes on in a local Body of Believers is but the rippling surface of a vast reservoir of experiences that shape the congregants, color their perceptions, and influence their actions.

After lying in ruins for a hundred years following its destruction by the Romans, Corinth was rebuilt by Julius Caesar in 46 B.C. as a Roman colony where veterans could retire. It was located on a narrow isthmus tying the southern part of Greece to the north, and all land traffic passed through it. More important, it was better for ships to haul their cargo over its 4-mile land bridge than risk the perilous 200-mile journey around treacherous Cape Malea.

Because of its strategic location and commercial importance, Corinth soon became one of the wealthiest and most socially diverse cities of the ancient world. It attracted people of every nationality and religion. In that most residents were transplants from somewhere else and thus free from traditional familial and cultural constraints, they did as they pleased.

Religious life in Corinth reflected this spirit of disconnectedness. Like Athens to the north, theirs was a city "full of idols" and "objects of worship" (Acts 17:16, 23), one for every taste and temperament. Mystery religions were popular. Through sacrificial rites and secret knowledge, devotees believed they could achieve a mystical union with the gods. In a state of spiritual ecstasy, they would sometimes speak an unintelligible tongue believed to be the language of the gods. It is not surprising that new converts would import this experience into Christian worship (see 1 Corinthians 14). Such practices led to highly privatized religious experiences. After all, who needs written Scriptures and a worshiping community when devotees can enter into "the realm of the gods" entirely on their own, without the constraints and demands of communal responsibilities?

Parallels between first-century Corinth and today's self-indulgent culture are immediately obvious. In addition, many Christians today misapply Martin Luther's foundational Reformation doctrine of "salvation by grace through

faith alone" to mean "*alone* and *apart* from the Church." We
see evidence of this on every hand. Evangelistic appeals often invite people to "receive Christ, *not* join the church." The
ever-popular doctrine of eternal security teaches that one's
eternal salvation has everything to do with Christ and nothing to do with the Church. Thanks to the wonders of our
multimedia age, all one needs to be spiritually nourished is
an easy chair, reading glasses, and a remote control.

Ours is not the first generation of believers to say, "I
don't need the Church." Like U-2's lead singer, Bono—who
has been involved in a loosely structured Christian fellowship, prays, says grace before meals, and has a favorite Bible
translation—many believe that "organized religion gets in
the way of meeting God."[1] The title of Philip Yancey's best-
seller, *Soul Survivor: How My Faith Survived the Church*, implies that the Church is not the answer, but the problem.

THE CHURCH: VISIBLE AND INVISIBLE

Many who keep their distance from the demands and
messiness of actual local church involvement believe with
Augustine that there are two Churches—one spiritual and
the other physical. There is a major problem with this notion
of an invisible Church—it doesn't exist. We can no more
separate the "spiritual church" from real people in actual congregations than we can separate the human spirit from the
physical body. The only Church that the New Testament
knows is concrete gatherings of believers.

It is clear that the "gifts of the Spirit" of which Paul
speaks in 1 Corinthians 12:1-11 are communal in nature.
"The manifestation of the Spirit" is not for private edification only, but "is given for *the common good*" (v. 7, emphasis
added). There is a cooperative relationship between the individual and the community. One's spiritual gift can neither be
realized nor expressed apart from the community, and the
community is totally dependent upon the "gifts of the Spirit"

of its members, exercised for enlightenment, edification, encouragement, and enablement of the whole body (vv. 8-11, 27-30; see Ephesians 4:11-16).

AN INDISPENSABLE UNITY

"Apart from the Church, there is no salvation," declared Cyprian, the influential third-century church father. That statement is not dogmatic, but profoundly true. "What life have you that is not in community," asked the poet T. S. Eliot, "and what community not lived in the praise of God?"

We do not know how many heard Peter's powerful sermon on the Day of Pentecost and believed on Jesus in their hearts. All the Scriptures tell us about are those who "accepted his message," stepped out of the unbelieving crowd to be "baptized," and then faithfully "devoted themselves to the apostles' teaching and to the fellowship, to the breaking of bread and to prayer" (Acts 2:41-42). Apart from that tangible community of believers, and those who have faithfully followed in their footsteps across the centuries, we would never have heard about Jesus. Much less would nearly 2 billion people around the world gather every Lord's day to confess with glad and generous hearts that "Jesus Christ is Lord, to the glory of God the Father" (Philippians 2:11).

A BOLD CLAIM

If Paul's assertion that "God was pleased to have all his fullness dwell in [Jesus]" (Colossians 1:19) was scandalous to Jews and craziness to Gentiles in his day, how much more so today? How can anything as feeble, frail, and flaky as the typical church—a mixed bag of saints and sinners, believers and hypocrites, selfless servants and whackos—possibly be the "Body of Christ"? To speak of the stodgy church on the corner of Elm and Main as the real "Body of Christ" is pious nonsense to many.

And yet, that is exactly what Paul says. It was not to

some obscure entity floating in outer space, but to actual congregations of believers in Corinth that he addressed these words: "For we were all baptized *by one Spirit* into *one body.* . . . Now *you* [collectively] are the body of Christ, and *each one of you* is a part of it" (1 Corinthians 12:13, 27, emphasis added). This astonishing insight was not the result of mature reflection, but instant revelation. After falling to the ground on the road to Damascus, he heard the voice of Christ Alive saying, "Saul, Saul, why do you persecute me?" (Acts 9:4).

Paul made a profound discovery that day. The risen Christ so identifies with those who follow in His footsteps that to persecute the Church is to wound Him as well. Here is the stark and somewhat scary truth: *how a person treats the Church is how he or she treats Christ.*

So, where is Jesus present in the world? In "His Body" the Church—"warts and all." The living Christ makes himself known, not through some sort of privatized spiritual osmosis, but in human packages—the voices, hands, hearts, and hugs of living and breathing people. Were it not for such churches and the sacrificial devotion of its members, my friend Roger would not have at his disposal a Bible, gospel radio programs, Promise Keepers rallies, or truck-stop chapel services.

BROKEN PEOPLE, BROKEN BODY

It was hardly an exemplary congregation to which Paul wrote these letters. They had more problems per square inch than most churches today have per square yard. The Church, then and now, is not a museum of saints, but a hospital for sinners. It is composed of frail, fallible, and faulty human beings who are amazingly graced by God, and "called to be holy" (1 Corinthians 1:2). In order to join, we have to declare that we are unworthy to join.

We should not be surprised that the Church, which lives its life under the shadow of the Fall, bears the scars of sin's universal curse. When Jesus said, "This is my body which is broken for you" (1 Corinthians 11:24, KJV), He was not only pointing to His death, but was anticipating the day when His followers would carry on His ministry as His broken Body in the world, always and at every moment dependent upon Him for salvation, healing, and wholeness.

Ironically, it is the Church's very brokenness that draws broken people to Christ. The blockbuster film event of recent years was not Tim LaHaye's *Left Behind*, with its terrifying images of Jesus returning as the Cosmic Terminator who destroys His enemies, but Mel Gibson's *The Passion of the Christ*, with its heart-wrenching scenes of suffering love, and Jesus' anguished cry from the Cross, "Father, forgive them" (Luke 23:34). There is truth in the title of Ruth Graham's recent book, *In Every Pew Sits a Broken Heart*.

Yet, it is these very bruised and battered people, lifting up soiled hands and hurting hearts to God, that constitute the authentic expression of Christ's ongoing presence in the world. Though the Church is fractured with chasms wide and deep, the living Christ is still pleased to own this fragmented Body as His own. Or as Paul put it, though "its parts are many, they form *one* body" (1 Corinthians 12:12, emphasis added).

SO, WHY GET INVOLVED?

First, a Christian's *survival depends upon the Church.* Even as a hand or foot cut off from the human body dies, so does the individual who cuts himself or herself off from the spiritual and social nourishment of a tangible Body of Believers. There is an unmistakable life-generating and spirit-enhancing chemistry that takes place when two or three—or two or three thousand—believers gather together for the express purpose of lifting up the name of Jesus. Even as campfire coals burn brighter and longer when crowded together, so do believers. Though it seems to defy the laws of physics, four strands of rope bound tightly together are not *four* times stronger than each individual strand, but *sixteen* times.

It is true that many who have once been a part of the Body of Christ may be able to "talk the talk" and "walk the walk" with the most conscientious churchperson. Nevertheless, they are like twigs that my wife has cut off trees for flower arrangements; they have maintained their form for years, but have yet to sprout a leaf or grow an orange.

Second, *the Church's survival depends upon the Christian.* Deprived of a hand or a foot, the human body is immeasurably crippled. If enough body parts are cut off, the body dies.

Not long after Kathleen Norris had undergone a midlife conversion and had joined the small, country church where her grandmother had worshiped for 60 years, she became increasingly frustrated with the pettiness and crankiness of the people. She began to wonder if she wouldn't be better off cultivating her spiritual life on her own.

As she was mulling this over one Sunday morning, the pastor preached on Mark 6:30-34, where Jesus and His disciples detoured from their intended place of retreat to tend to the desperate needs of the "sheep without a shepherd" that had followed them. "We go to church," the pastor said, "for other people, because someone may need you there."

That statement jolted her. "I stopped doodling on my bulletin," she says, "and began to pay attention. . . . It may do someone good just to see my face, or share a conversation over coffee before the worship service."[2]

A PASSIONATE LOVE AFFAIR

If we were to list all the valid reasons why we should "not give up meeting together, as some are in the habit of doing" (Hebrews 10:25), they would pale into insignificance compared to the one reason Paul gives us. "Christ *loved* the church and gave himself up for her" (Ephesians 5:25, emphasis added). To love Jesus is, quite simply, to love what He loves. And He loves the Church so deeply and intensely that He gave up His life for her in the ultimate demonstration of self-giving, sacrificial love. Jesus gave only one "new command," and it was directed specifically to His disciples: "Love one another. *As I have loved you, so you must love one another*" (John 13:34, emphasis added). We cannot love in isolation, but only in community.

Paul's use of the human body as a metaphor to describe the Church is immediately followed by the most eloquent love poem ever written. The "love" of which Paul speaks in 1 Corinthians 13 is not *eros*, the privatized self-love that characterizes our godless sensual culture. Nor is it *phileo*, an abstract benevolent feeling for all the peoples of the world. Rather, it is *agape*, self-giving and self-sacrificing love for real people, beginning with our families and those who make up the Body of Christ, into which God in His gracious providence has placed us. And it is God, Paul tells us, who is always at work incorporating us as individual members into His collective Body, always at work fitting us in where our gifts and abilities will be maximized, and in those places where our resources are most needed (see 1 Corinthians 12:11, 18, 24, 28). Such love is "not self-seeking" (1 Corinthians 13:5), but always other-directed.

The man who passionately loves his wife does not need to be lectured about the necessity of spending time with her, nor does he need to be told to work with all his might in order that her every need is fulfilled. So it is for the one who has fallen deeply in love with Jesus. For such a one, pouring time, money, and energy into the Church is not a burden, but an ever-increasing joy. If he or she has a quarrel with the Church, it is always a "lover's quarrel." Commitment to the relationship "until death do us part" is never in doubt.

Our four-year-old daughter ran across the living room one evening while I was reading in my comfortable easy chair. With a flying leap, she crashed into me with enough force to knock my book out of my hands and my glasses off my head. Before I could respond with an appropriate father-ly rebuke, she threw her arms around my neck and said, "Daddy, will you please love me?"

Scratch the surface in anybody's church, large or small, and there you will find someone crying out, "Will you please love me?" The secret of the abundant life is capsuled in one short saying of Jesus: "For whoever wants to save his life will lose it, but whoever loses his life for me will find it" (Matthew 16:25). And what better way to "lose our lives" than in the service of Christ's body, the Church?

A depressed American soldier, imprisoned in Burma by the Japanese during World War II, experienced a profound spiritual conversion that eventually led to the transformation of that jungle camp for both prisoners and guards. His testimony consisted of three short sentences:

I sought my God, but my God I could not see.
I sought myself, but my self eluded me.
I sought my brother and found all three.

Notes:

1. *Christianity Today*, January 2005, 45.
2. Kathleen Norris, *Amazing Grace: A Vocabulary of Faith* (New York: Riverhead Books, 1998), 203-04.

Scripture Cited: Matthew 16:25; Luke 23:34; John 13:34; Acts 2:41-42; 9:4; 17:16, 23; 1 Corinthians 1:2; 11:24; 12:1-13, 18, 24, 27-28; 13:5; Ephesians 5:25; Philippians 2:11; Colossians 1:19; Hebrews 10:25

About the Author: Dr. Cowles is retired from teaching at Northwest Nazarene University, and currently is an adjunct professor at Point Loma Nazarene University's School of Religion and Christian Ministry.

WHATEVER I WANT!

BY EVERETT LEADINGHAM

From: DISCIPLE@21STCENTURY.CHURCH

To: PAUL@APOSTLES.CHRIST

Subject: Lunch

Dear Brother Paul,

The other day I went out to lunch with a business colleague. We went to a popular restaurant downtown. As we were coming out after lunch, we ran into a member of the church where I attend. He was offended and said that Christians should not go into a place like that.

When I saw him at church later in the week, I tried to explain that my colleague had chosen the restaurant, and I had to go along with her in order to secure the contract for our company. He didn't accept that.

Since "everything is permissible," as the saying goes, why does he have a problem with where I eat lunch?

A Concerned Believer

Probably most people in churches today will not understand the question raised by the E-mail above. For them, eating food "offered to an idol" (1 Corinthians 10:19) is a dead
issue. It has faded away like the horse and buggy or legalism.

For those who do not profess to live by the standards of
the Church, this will seem like a non-issue as well. They live
by the motto, "I'm an adult; I'll do whatever I want!" So they
wouldn't think twice (probably not even once) about which
restaurant they eat in.

Nevertheless, is 1 Corinthians 10 really a passage of
scripture with no relevance for our lives today?

It has been an issue at least twice in my time within the
Church. Once, the question arose when my wife went to
lunch with a friend from church. Their workplaces were near
each other in the small town where we lived. Once in a while
they would go to lunch together at a local restaurant that
was also a bar. This establishment had a reputation for making two delicious dishes that my wife and her friend dearly
loved—open-faced, hot roast beef sandwiches and home-
made chicken and noodles. Someone from church saw them
exiting the "bar" and said something similar to "Christians
shouldn't go into a place like that."

Not long after that, a controversy arose in our Sunday
School class. It was getting close to Christmas, and we wanted to have a party. As the class discussed possibilities, someone suggested a particular restaurant where we could rent a
private room for our party. That seemed like a good idea to
most class members. Most, but not all. A small group did
not like the choice of that restaurant because they also sold
liquor there. They did not feel our church group should
spend our money in such a place, even though we would not
be drinking alcohol ourselves.

We might still be tempted to say that those are not issues any more in the Church. However, before we dismiss
them as irrelevant, maybe we should think a little harder
about the effect our behavior has on other Christians.

The town where I live now has many restaurants that are described as "upscale." Most of the Christians I know enjoy going to them, especially for business lunches and special occasions. All of these restaurants have bars in them, though none of the Christians I know consume any of their alcohol. Some of the customers in these high-class places are prostitutes and homosexuals, though none of the Christians I know are looking to hook up with such persons. Does being in these particular restaurants mean that Christians drink wine and condone immoral sexual liaisons that might happen there? Could our guilt by association be assumed?

We would probably say that being there does not mean any of that. We would most likely agree with the saying that seemed common in Corinth, "Everything is permissible" (1 Corinthians 10:23). Paul himself agreed with that on one level, but he saw danger in it on another level. He agreed that Christ had set them free from the restrictions of Jewish law. Yet, he saw that in that freedom they might be condoning some activities incompatible with proper Christian conduct. And most importantly, they seemed to be selfish. Paul wanted to help them find a proper balance of enjoying freedom in Christ without harming the community of faith.

In 1 Corinthians 10, Paul talks about three situations to help us understand Christian freedom: learning from history, trying to exist in two incompatible worlds, and influencing the faith of others.

HISTORY TEACHES US

We can learn valuable lessons from history, *if* we are aware of history and *if* we heed the lessons.

Any time a person goes to a new doctor or is admitted to a hospital, the medical personnel will ask a series of questions designed to ascertain the person's medical history. Not only what has happened to the patient in the past will help the doctor with the present illness, but the family medical history is important as well. If parents or siblings have suffered from particular diseases, doctors know the current patient's propensities. The wise person takes his or her family history of disease into account when making food and lifestyle decisions. Either forgetting or not knowing the history can have detrimental effects on a person's current and future health.

The apostle Paul opened chapter 10 of his first letter to the Corinthians with a reminder of their history and its lessons for them. Interestingly, Paul begins by talking about "our forefathers" (v. 1). The phrase seems curious when we consider the makeup of the Corinthian church. They were not all Jews. Corinth was a Greek city, and the congregation no doubt reflected the diversity of the community. Still, Paul talks about the spirit of Christ—the eternally existent Son of God—being present in the Israelites' exodus from Egypt. Paul saw Christianity as a continuation of salvation history. Gentiles who had become Christians had become "Israel," the people of God (see Romans 11). Paul had taught this when he was at Corinth, so he knew they would understand themselves as coming from Jewish forefathers in the faith.

For Paul, there was a purpose for reminding the Corinthians of the religious heritage. "These things occurred as examples to keep us from setting our hearts on evil things" (v. 6). Paul's first applied lesson was: don't join pagan parties, because they worship idols. Even worse, they include immoral sexual behavior. Paul's quotation of Exodus 32:6 reflects his understanding of how "revelry" went. In Paul's day, pagan temples and Roman-style banquets included sex as part of their festivities. So any Christians who attended either temples or banquets would be confronted with doing things he or she should not be doing.

The second lesson Paul lifted up from history was: don't test God's patience nor complain. Verse 9 alludes to the story of Numbers 21:5ff., and verse 10 refers to incidents recorded in Numbers 14:2, 36; 16:41-49. In both cases, the forefathers suffered dire consequences for their behavior.

However, the messages Paul highlighted from history were not all negative. He was not trying to drive the Corinthians to despair. Rather, he reminded them that God was still on their side. The Exodus had not been an easy experience for the Israelites. The 40 years of wandering in the wilderness had been stressful—full of fatigue, hunger, and even death. However in the Exodus, God had provided them a way out of oppressive slavery. In all the forms of temptation that enticed the Corinthian Christians, none was unusual for the human race. Nor would any temptation cause God to be unfaithful. No matter how difficult the pressure to sin became, God would always provide them a way out, another exodus from oppression.

IS THE FOOD SPOILED?

In verse 14, Paul repeats an injunction: "flee from idolatry." Then he proceeds through verse 22 to explain why he must emphasize this, this time not with predictions of dire consequences but by appeals to the Corinthians' sensibleness. In the last part of this chapter, he will allow some wiggle room in the where-can-Christians-eat-lunch debate, but here he absolutely forbids Christians to eat in the pagan temples. Why?

The reason is at the heart of what it means to be "in Christ." The Lord's Supper is not just another meal, not just an ordinary gathering of believers. Rather, partaking of the Lord's Supper is literally communing with the Lord, taking part in His life and death, becoming one with Jesus. Eating the "body and blood" of Christ is a defining moment, an identification as His true follower.

The meal consumed in a pagan temple is not an ordinary meal either. Though Paul rightfully points out that neither idols nor sacrifices to them are in any way real in terms of salvation, those who participate are acknowledging the same things as Christians in the Lord's Supper. Pagan rituals

included the belief that the god to whom the meat was sacrificed was present and entered the person who ate, giving him
or her all the supposed benefits that characterized the god.

This sets up an impossible situation for Christians: "You
cannot partake of the table of the Lord and the table of de-
mons" (v. 21, NRSV). Or as Paul put it in the other Corinthian letter, "What do righteousness and wickedness have in
common?" (2 Corinthians 6:14). Jesus said such an attempt-
ed alliance between good and evil will have dire consequences. "A house divided against itself will fall" (Luke
11:17). One writer explained it to our generation this way:
"It was true in Corinth and it is true today, that the [one]
who has handled the sacred things of Christ cannot soil his
[or her] hands with mean and unworthy things."*

Food that has been offered as a sacrifice to a false god is
spoiled food for Christians. To ingest it would taint their
identity as Christians. No wonder Paul was so strongly
against going to pagan temples and participating in pagan
revelries.

DINNER AT MY FRIEND'S HOUSE

Still, Paul knew that Christians got invited to their
friends' homes for dinner. Sometimes their friends were fellow Christians; sometimes they were unbelievers. Either way,
the invited Christian had no way of knowing whether the
meat for the meal had been purchased at a butcher shop sup-
plied by a pagan temple or not. And Paul also knew that
some of those invitations were business lunches, and involved going to restaurants where they might be serving
meat that had been offered to some idol. What did Paul say
about those situations?

His advice was simple: "Eat whatever is put before you"
(1 Corinthians 10:27). Don't ask questions. Eating a meal
with sacrificed meat in this case did not constitute participating in the sacrificial meal. In the environment of a private

home or a restaurant, there was no belief that eating the meat was taking in the characteristics of a god. In this case, meat was just meat. No one needed to know its origin.

However, if the host raised the question, Paul's advice was different. Don't eat if they raise a question. If the host says, "This meat came from the butcher shop by the idol's temple. I think it was probably used in the sacrifice there," just eat the vegetables. The very question means that the identification belief is on someone's mind. That means they are not sure if eating it will, in fact, conflict with their Christianity. Paul did not want any of the Christians to stray toward idolatry, so he prohibited eating under such circumstances.

For Paul, this was a matter of conscience—"the other man's conscience" (v. 29). This is a hard concept for 21st-century, individualistic Christians to grasp. The cohesiveness of the group as the community of faith was more important for Paul than any individual Christian within the group. That is why he wrote: "Now you are the body of Christ, and each one of you is a part of it" (1 Corinthians 12:27). "There is neither Jew nor Greek, slave nor free, male nor female, for you are all one in Christ Jesus" (Galatians 3:28). And he further advised Christians to "make every effort to keep the unity of the Spirit through the bond of peace" (Ephesians 4:3).

Paul knew that Christians were free in Christ, but he did not believe they should use their freedom selfishly. He acknowledged the common saying, but retained a sensible understanding. "'Everything is permissible'—but not everything is beneficial. 'Everything is permissible'—but not everything is constructive. Nobody should seek his own good, but the good of others" (1 Corinthians 10:23-24).

Apparently some of those in Corinth believed what people seem to think today: freedom is the right to do whatever they please, regardless of the consequences or the effect on others. Paul saw that there were limits to freedom. If someone's freedom in Christ caused someone else in the community of faith to stumble, then that person was not free to do whatever he or she wanted. The person who would be offended (or more realistically, confused) about his or her Christian faith by the other Christian exercising extreme freedom is the one who worried Paul. Confusion might weaken his or her faith, and thereby weaken the unity among the whole community of faith. This was not going in the right direction. Paul saw the goal of the community to be that "we all reach unity in the faith and in the knowledge of the Son of God and become mature, attaining to the whole measure of the fullness of Christ" (Ephesians 4:13).

We are, in fact, free. Not to do whatever we want, but to do what is right. We are free to be law-abiding citizens. We are free to seek the good of others. We are not free to be self-ish. And that is the important difference between an attitude of freedom that builds up and one that destroys. The more we think of ways to make our behavior have positive effects on others, the more freedom we enjoy as the community gets stronger and healthier. The more we ignore how our behavior has negative impact on others, the weaker and more un-healthy the group becomes. And this doesn't just apply to the Church. Society is affected in the same way. The more people think freedom is their right to be selfish, the weaker the fab-ric of society becomes, and the less free we all are.

RESPONSIBLE FREEDOM

The issues that were highlighted at the beginning of this chapter are often characterized as legalism. And "legal-ism" is a bad word among church folks. It conjures images of "Bible-thumpers" who dress in a particularly plain manner and frown a lot. No one wants to go back to those religiously oppressive days, including me.

However in 1 Corinthians 10, Paul is not advocating for a legalistic religion. Rather, he is lobbying for responsible freedom in Christ. He is suggesting that Christians think carefully about their actions so that no wrong signals are sent and that no one in the community of faith will be weakened. He wants Christians to do what is best for the entire group rather than what will please an individual's selfish desires. Paul is advocating a perspective like the one I learned as a child. The order of a Christian's priorities should be J-O-Y: Jesus, Others, You.

How does it work out when we follow Paul's directive, "Do not seek your own advantage, but that of the other" (v. 24, NRSV)? It works out quite nicely.

Remember the Sunday School class that was split over having a Christmas party at a restaurant that served liquor? Though the issue threatened to blow the class apart, it did not. After much prayer and long discussion, the class decided not to go to that restaurant in deference to the sensitivity of the other class members. Instead, we went to someone's home and had the first of many delightful parties over the years. In addition, the Holy Spirit used that issue to point the class in a new direction. Because of the prayer meetings and discussions sparked by the controversy, the class began to grow. In less than a year, the class grew from 5 people to averaging 70 each Sunday. Being sensitive to the conscience of others was the right decision because it honored God by honoring the community of faith.

And the question about whether my wife and her friend should eat at the restaurant/bar had a happy ending too. The person who complained realized that it was not a big deal. They were not "sacrificing to idols" by eating there. That person knew the food was good at that place, and nothing else was going on there. So my wife and her friend continued to enjoy the roast beef sandwiches and chicken and noodles.

I think it boils down to this: Don't violate your conscience or your faith community's standards for the sake of personal gain. Light and darkness can't mix. "You cannot serve both God and Money" (Matthew 6:24). It only becomes a problem if someone else in the church brings it up because they do not feel as free in Christ as you do. In that case, be sensitive enough to do what will strengthen the faith of the entire community.

If business takes you somewhere you wouldn't go on your own, and being there does not involve you in "pagan revelries," relax and enjoy yourself. I hope you sign a lucrative contract and can increase your tithe tenfold.

Notes:

*William Barclay, *The Letters to the Corinthians* (Philadelphia: The Westminster Press, 1956), 103.

Scripture Cited: Numbers 14:2, 36; 16:41-49; 21:5ff.; Matthew 6:24; Luke 11:17; 1 Corinthians 10:1-33; 2 Corinthians 6:14; Galatians 3:28; Ephesians 4:3, 13

About the Author: Dr. Leadingham is editor of the Dialog Series and executive editor for the adult curriculum group of the Church of the Nazarene, Kansas City, Missouri.

WHETHER MARRIED OR SINGLE

BY GERARD REED

From: DISCIPLE@21STCENTURY.CHURCH

To: PAUL@APOSTLES.CHRIST

Subject: Sex and Marriage

Dear Brother Paul,

I think you would agree that we live in a culture obsessed with sex. And the divorce rate seems to be growing. Some in the Church say that marriage is necessary for all Christians in order to be sexually pure. Others say that marriage doesn't protect us any better. How can Christians live pure lives in today's cultural climate?

A Concerned Believer

Questions concerning sex and marriage are troubling the Church these days. Though lifelong, heterosexual marriage has apparently been the norm for believers for 20 centuries, we now live in a radically different world, where lots of people no longer see marriage and family as particularly important. Family, for many of us, simply means the group of friends with whom we like to hang out.

Maybe marriage isn't really important. America's marriage rate has dropped by 40 percent since 1970, and many people thrive as singles, cohabiting when it suits them, pursuing careers, retaining their personal independence. They believe we don't really need a spouse to live well. Yet, women "shacking up" with men suffer extreme violence five times more often than their married counterparts. And the illegitimacy rate has soared, so that one of every three babies enters a single, female-headed home. This probably harms children, since they are twice as likely to be abused as children of married couples. And it does seem that children whose parents divorce suffer.

For many, sexual freedom tops the list of what they want from life. Their thinking goes something like this:

Our right to sexual freedom and privacy has been established as a preeminent value by our nation's highest court. And it's a career, not marriage, that enables one to make the money needed to live the "good life" with posh apartments and cool cars. Changing economics and our technological world require a new morality with values we create, not ideals imposed upon us by old men in past dark ages. Sex, after all, is mainly intended for pleasure, isn't it? Therefore, whatever gives us pleasure is obviously good. So long as no one gets hurt, so long as two people really love each other, what's wrong with "shacking up"? When a husband and wife no longer enjoy being married, what's wrong with divorcing and finding others who really love them? And since sex and love make life more meaningful for same-sex couples, what's wrong with homosexuals marrying? If two people really love each other and want to express their love sexually, who's to say that it's necessary to marry or stay married or limit sex to the opposite sex?

If Christians are tempted to accept those ideas, we should look at what the Scriptures teach us.

ARE THESE QUESTIONS NEW?

Twenty years after Jesus' resurrection, Christians in Corinth wrote Paul a letter asking various questions about such things as sex and marriage. To understand his response in 1 Corinthians 7, we must sketch the cultural context, the Roman Empire in the first century A.D.

Within every culture there resides both the hard rock of human nature and the shifting sands of custom. Given that God created us (male and female) in His very image, and noting that everything He created is "good" or "very good," all discussion of sex and marriage must be rooted in the realities of human nature. Declaring that "it is not good that man should be alone," God gave Eve to Adam as a "helper comparable to him" (Genesis 2:18, NKJV). Accordingly, God's first command for the first couple was quite clear: "Be fruitful and increase in number; fill the earth and subdue it" (1:28).

Traditional Jews lived out this mandate. Men were virtually obligated to marry, generally around the age of 18. "If a man did not marry and have children, he was said to have 'slain his posterity, . . . to have lessened the image of God in the world.'"[1] Men were expected to follow the strict sexual code set forth in the Hebrew Scriptures that called for the monogamous marriages that enable fathers and mothers to rightly rear children and prohibited nonmarital sexual activities that threatened family well-being—fornication, adultery, incest, sodomy, and bestiality.

Rightly discerned, our very nature prescribes coupling—a man and a woman sexually uniting—and procreation. As Aristotle noted: "Between man and wife friendship seems to exist by nature; for man is naturally inclined to form couples —even more than to form cities, inasmuch as the household is earlier and more necessary than the city" and reproduction is a drive humans have in common with animals.[2] So Paul, writing to the Corinthians, reminded them that we, by nature, crave friendship and enjoy sex, something designed for our good, one of God's greatest gifts.

Yet, just as Eden's first couple revolted against God as Sovereign Lord, their descendents have revolted against their own nature. In the most basic sense, sin is the prideful

refusal to accept our true nature as human beings designed
to serve and worship God. Thus, history records our ances-
tors' refusal to follow the blueprint inscribed in their very
genes. And they devised nonnatural ways to indulge their
sexual appetites.

THE WORLD PAUL LIVED IN

In the first-century Greco-Roman world, many folks
despised marriage and family. The Greeks widely celebrated
health and the beauty of the human body; so, stylish women
preferred not to bear children lest they lose their alluring fig-
ures. Roman historians, including Livy and Tacitus, often
lamented the moral decline evident in the collapse of strong
families into the sexual looseness of the empire. Augustus
Caesar, reigning emperor when Christ was born, noted this
and tried to mandate chastity and childbearing. Yet, his own
daughter Julia led the way in openly defying the emperor's
edicts!

Augustus's successor, Tiberius (in power when Christ
was crucified), was notorious for his sexual perversions. On
the island of Capri, he indulged his appetite for pornography
and unnatural sex. He even conscripted children to abuse in
pedophilia.

Under Tiberius's successor, Caligula, things got even
worse. Rather than orgies restricted to the island of Capri,
they pervaded the city of Rome. Caligula lived incestuously
with his sisters, who sat with him and his wife at public banquets. He ordered husbands and wives to divorce so as to
briefly "marry" whichever woman amused him at the moment. To raise imperial revenues, Caligula opened a brothel
in his palace.

The next emperor, Claudius, though far more restrained
and circumspect than Caligula, suffered with a wife named
Valeria Messalina, whose sexual escapades included a public
coupling with one of her lovers in the presence of a large

company of banqueters! Then came Nero, who brought whores and dancing girls to the imperial palace. Nero abused boys and seduced married women. He even castrated and "married" a young boy, whom he dressed up as a woman and took with him on his travels about the empire.

First-century Romans, following their leaders, not only engaged in promiscuous sex, but they also married and divorced routinely. Some Romans had dozens of husbands or wives. Marriages were consummated and then abandoned for financial or political reasons, and sacred vows were little more than passing formalities. Although Jews generally had a higher view of marriage than their pagan counterparts, they, too, regularly resorted to divorce. A woman could leave her husband by informing the community elders that she had been deceived as a young woman and wanted a divorce. Childless couples were free to separate after a few years, since having children was considered essential. Subsequent to divorce, both partners were free to find other spouses.

Yet, paradoxically, sexual laxity was not the only position espoused in the first century. Whereas emperors flaunted all standards and engaged in immoral behaviors, others in the Greco-Roman world insisted that neither sexual relations nor even marriage were truly good for a person. They celebrated celibacy. To be pure involved abstaining from all sexual relations. Certain ancient thinkers considered marriage "a necessary evil." Epictetus, a Greek Stoic who spent his life in Rome, considered his job as a teacher too important to compromise by marrying and having children. Though traditional Jews robustly embraced the married estate, some of them in the time of Christ—notably the Essenes—rejected family life as too worldly and established monastic communities near the Dead Sea. Intensely religious, anticipating the end of the world, they renounced marriage so as to live perfectly pure lives in accord with the Jewish Law.

PAUL'S RESPONSE

Given this broader background, we can better understand the issues at Corinth in about A.D. 55. The city's recently established Christian congregation had serious problems. "It is," Paul wrote, "actually reported that there is
sexual immorality among you, and of a kind that does not
occur even among pagans: A man has his father's wife"
(1 Corinthians 5:1). Paul declared that such must not be!
Indeed a Christian must "flee sexual immorality," for "your
body is the temple of the Holy Spirit" and one should "glorify God in your body and in your spirit, which are God's"
(6:18-20, NKJV).

With chastity as the Christian norm for sexual behavior,
Paul responded to questions concerning marriage, celibacy,
and divorce. Marriage is certainly a good estate, natural and
necessary for most people. A man and a woman, united for a
lifetime, enter a holy relationship that allows them to enjoy
sexual satisfaction, establish families wherein children are accepted as a blessing, and celebrate the glory of God as the
Creator of all good things. Paul's training as a rabbi certainly
alerted him to the fact that Jewish men were expected to
marry in their late teens. Husbands and wives, in a profound
sense, belong to each other. They should cater to each other's
needs and provide the sexual satisfaction men and women
naturally crave.

Once married, people should stay married! Jesus had
made this perfectly clear, saying: "Haven't you read . . . that at
the beginning the Creator 'made them male and female,' and
said, 'For this reason a man will leave his father and mother
and be united to his wife, and the two will become one flesh'?
So they are no longer two, but one. Therefore what God has
joined together, let man not separate" (Matthew 19:4-6).

For the unmarried, however, Paul said—writing "as a
concession, not as a command" (1 Corinthians 7:6) to make
clear that he sets forth his personal position—it may be bet-

ter not to marry. This enables a person to devote himself or herself more totally to Christ and His church. Especially in times of persecution and stress, single persons are freer than married couples with children to risk lives and property for their faith. Within the providence of God, some should sense a calling to remain unmarried, to be celibate in order to better serve and glorify God.

THREE PRINCIPLES FOR CHRISTIANS

In light of this biblical passage, what conclusions shall we draw? At least three principles seem evident: (1) chastity is the Christian norm, (2) marriage is good, (3) celibacy is also good.

First, chastity—restricting all sexual activity to married couples—is the norm for Christians. C. S. Lewis noted insightfully, "Chastity is the most unpopular of the Christian virtues. There is no getting away from it: the old Christian rule is, 'Either marriage, with complete faithfulness to one partner, or else total abstinence.'"[3] The bitter fruit of promiscuity is clearly documented. Meg Meeker, a medical doctor who practiced pediatric and adolescent medicine for 20 years, watched the '60s sexual revolution usher in an epidemic of sexually transmitted diseases (STD). In 1960, syphilis and gonorrhea were the two STDs that concerned physicians. Forty years later, there are dozens of them—perhaps 100—and some have no known cure. "Every day, 8,000 teens will become infected with a new STD."[4] Of the sexually active teens, fully one-fourth carry a STD. A British study indicates "that almost half of all girls are likely to become infected with an STD during their very first sexual experience."[5] Such are the results, Meeker declares, of the sexual revolution. "With the coming of that revolution, my own generation demanded previously unheard-of sexual freedom and promiscuity. We may have gotten what we thought we wanted, but the ride wasn't free. Countless children are now paying the price."[6] Epidemic paints a bleak portrait! What little hope there is for our kids, as one might expect, comes from better parenting. The clearly missing standard in our culture is chastity! To be Christ's representative on earth, we must insist it's the only right way to live.

Second, marriage is good. This is evident in the thesis of a book by Glenn Stanton: "First-time, lifelong, monogamous marriage is the relationship that best provides for the most favorable exercise of human sexuality, the overall well-being of adults, and the proper socialization of children."[7] Marriage is simply the best setting for human flourishing.

Tragically, this best of all relationships has been ruthlessly assailed and thoughtlessly neglected. "The decline of marriage and the breakup of the family is unquestionably our most pressing problem."[8] It worries those who study our society. "At no time in history, with the possible exception of Imperial Rome, has the institution of marriage been more problematic than it is today."[9] As one collegian declared, "The sexual revolution is over and everyone lost."[10] Everyone lost because folks believed a great lie! The truth is that good sex binds together married men and women, that virginity before marriage is the best way to prepare for it, and that very traditional sexual standards enable men and women to live wisely and well. Yet, we allow movies and TV and women's magazines and soft-porn publications to peddle their untruths to unsupervised youngsters, who fall prey to the notion that sexual satisfaction abounds in nightly "hook-ups" and uncommitted "relationships."

"What children need most is for their parents to be and remain married."[11] Fathers, especially, are essential. Children need more than adults—even caring adults—in a house. They need their moms and dads. This means, of course, that we must somehow reverse the divorce rate. Adults who divorce may gain some relief from their problems, some improvement in their satisfaction with life, but their gains are usually purchased with their children's pain!

Third, Paul urges us to acknowledge the value of celibacy. He called upon the unmarried in Corinth to take advantage of their singleness to better serve the Lord. Similarly, Jesus praised those who "have renounced marriage because of the kingdom of heaven" (Matthew 19:12). In subsequent centuries, many believers followed Paul's admonition to consecrate themselves purely to God. All pleasures, however proper in themselves, can deflect one's attention from higher goods. So, the pleasures, and obligations, of marriage can simply consume so much of one's time that little remains to invest in caring for eternal things.

With chastity—restricting all sexual activity to married couples—as the norm for Christians, today's Church has the answers it needs to navigate the murky waters of the surrounding culture. Christ calls all kinds of people into His church. What we must do is serve God—whether married or single—and serve Him always with pure hearts and surrendered lives.

Notes:

1. William Barclay, *Letters to the Corinthians* (Philadelphia: The Westminster Press, 1956), 68.

2. W. D. Ross, trans., *The Nicomachean Ethics of Aristotle* (Oxford: The Clarendon Press, 1908), VIII:12 [Accessed at www.sacred-texts.com].

3. C. S. Lewis, *Mere Christianity* (New York: Touchstone, 1996), 75.

4. Meg Meeker, *Epidemic: How Teen Sex Is Killing Our Kids* (Washington, D.C.: LifeLine Press, 2002), 3.

5. Meeker, 12.

6. Meeker, 33.

7. Glenn T. Stanton, *Why Marriage Matters: Reasons to Believe in Marriage in Postmodern Society* (Colorado Springs: Pinon Press, 1997), 11.

8. Stanton, 18.

9. Kingsley Davis, quoted in Stanton, 25.

10. Stanton, 34.

11. Stanton, 100.

Scripture Cited: Genesis 1:28; 2:18; Matthew 19:4-6, 12; 1 Corinthians 5:1; 6:18-20; 7:6

About the Author: Dr. Reed is a professor in the School of Theology and Christian Ministry and chaplain at Point Loma
Nazarene University, San Diego, California.

CAN
WE
ALL AGREE?

BY CASEY DAVIS

From: DISCIPLE@21STCENTURY.CHURCH

To: PAUL@APOSTLES.CHRIST

Subject: Disagreements

Dear Brother Paul,

I don't understand what's going on. I love going to my church. I love the people there. But there's so much conflict! We argue over how to decorate the sanctuary at Christmas and how many services to have at Easter. Some people want to expand the size of the building, while others want to buy new property and build a whole new facility. Others say we're fine the way we are. People who have no gifts for leadership try to run every committee, and others who do have the gifts get pushed into the background. There are broken families who are made to feel like second-class citizens. Those with more money are more easily heard than those with less. The church tries to take a stand on social issues, but there's nothing close to agreement.

> *You wrote a lot about unity in the Body of Christ. You spoke as if there already was this unity, but you also commanded us to work for and achieve it. As I look at your letters, I see as many problems then as I do now. The biggest thing I hear non-Christians saying about the Church (other than that it's filled with hypocrites) is that we can't get along with one another. How do we get rid of all this bickering?*
>
> *A Concerned Believer*

Paul considered unity among believers to be one of the most important distinctives of the Christian life. It is a major focus in the letters to the Galatians, Ephesians, and Corinthians, and is the controlling theme in Philippians. Ephesians 4:1, in fact, has strong similarities to Philippians 1:27, where Paul says, "Whatever happens, conduct yourselves in a manner worthy of the gospel of Christ. Then, whether I come and see you or only hear about you in my absence, I will know that you stand firm in *one spirit*, contending as *one man* for the faith of the gospel" (emphasis added). In both cases, Paul is wrapping up everything that he has just said and introducing the major point of the rest of the letter to the Ephesians, a command to proper conduct which centers on unity in the Body of Christ.

Paul spends the first three chapters of Ephesians presenting God's eternal plan to bring all of humanity together under the headship of Christ. Beginning at 4:1 and continuing through 6:20, he "urges" ("begs," NRSV) his audience "to live a life worthy of [their] calling." One writer states, "Behavior is thus seen in Ephesians as both response to what God has done in Christ, and as the proper accompaniment to the praise of God, the two themes present in chapters 1-3."*

Living a worthy life involves, first of all, "[making] every effort to keep the unity of the Spirit" (4:3). Note that Christians are not to *create* unity. Paul has stressed in the first three chapters that only Jesus could do that—and He has done it. All things are under His headship (see 1:7-10, 18-23; 2:6, 13-18; 3:10-12). Our job is to *keep* ("maintain," NRSV) that unity which Christ has sacrificed himself to achieve. Thus, our part is to carry on that which Jesus has not only called us to, but enabled us to do.

A friend of mine was traveling in Israel when his car broke down. As the mechanic repaired the car, he listened to the engine. When it was just right, he exclaimed in Hebrew, "Righteous!" An engine can be righteous when it performs as it was designed to perform. The same holds true for humans.

Just as we can only be righteous when we live as God created us to live, so we can only have unity when we follow the One who created that unity, the One who is himself both unified and unique. Note the use of a Trinitarian formula in 4:4-6 as Paul speaks of "one Spirit," "one Lord" (a common designation for Paul in referring to Jesus), "one God and Father." We don't need to spend a lot of time and effort to unify the Body of Christ. Instead, we need to focus on Christ and the tasks that He has given us. Then the unity that is already there will flourish.

MAINTAINING THE UNITY OF THE SPIRIT

Paul indicates what those tasks are when he moves immediately to a discussion of the gifts which Christ has given to the Church. Ephesians 4:11 gives one of five lists of gifts found in the New Testament (see also Romans 12:6-8; 1 Corinthians 12:8-10, 28-30; 1 Peter 4:10-11). What is particularly interesting about this list is that in naming only apostles, prophets, evangelists, pastors, and teachers, Paul is narrowing in on those who proclaim and teach the gospel. In speaking of unity, we might expect him to stress the gifts of serving (see Romans 12:7; 1 Peter 4:11); encouraging, contributing to the needs of others, and showing mercy (see Romans 12:8); or healing, helping, and administering (see 1 Corinthians 12:29). Helping other Christians out, making them feel good, and forgiving them for wrongs they have done to us are all good things. However, when it comes to maintaining that unity in the Body that only Christ can accomplish, Paul wants us to know that the crucial thing is proclaiming and teaching the very gospel that brought us together in the first place. The gospel is what distinguishes the Church from any other "organization."

These apostles, prophets, evangelists, pastors, and teachers "prepare God's people for works of service, so that the body of Christ may be built up" (Ephesians 4:12). Those who have been specifically gifted by God to proclaim and teach the gospel are a gift to the Church, not because they are the only ones who do the work, but because they equip others. When all of God's people are doing what God has called them to do, there is no room for disunity to creep into that unity which Christ has already established.

I grieve that so many churches no longer build and maintain their own buildings with volunteer labor. There are few things that bring a group of people together as closely as being involved in a construction project. I once asked two elderly sisters how they came to know Christ. They replied that their dad drove home from work every day past a property where men were building a church. Over time, he was so impressed with the camaraderie he saw that he decided to stop in and ask if he could help. In a short time, he developed a trusting relationship with those men, heard the gospel, and gave his heart to the Lord. The whole family ended up being saved.

There is nothing that will build up the Church like involving everyone in the shared mission. However, it is not enough just to be involved. Christ gave gifts so that the Body might be built up, not just in number, but "until we all reach unity in the faith and in the knowledge of the Son of God and become mature, attaining to the whole measure of the fullness of Christ" (4:13). Unity comes with knowledge and maturity *in the proclamation of the gospel*. It is tempting (as evidenced by the number of people who have done it) to point to 4:15 and say that the unity to which Paul is pointing in this passage can be created by being honest with one another in such a way that we hold up that person's best interests. First, we have already seen that unity cannot be *created*. We are called to *maintain* the unity which Christ sacrificed himself to accomplish. Second, speaking the truth in love is not trying to tell your spouse that he or she is fat without hurting his or her feelings. I have heard many people tell others difficult things in a caring manner and quote this verse. It is wonderful when a person can show true tough love for the benefit of another, but that is not what Paul is talking about here. (If you want a verse for that situation, go to 4:25.)

Biblical studies professors like to say, "Context is everything." When 4:15 is viewed in its context, it is clear that the truth of which Paul is speaking is the gospel itself. Verse 13 speaks of the Christian goal of maturity, of the fullness of Christ. Paul contrasts this in verse 14 with the horrible thought of being like babies who are thrown about by "every wind of teaching and by the cunning and craftiness of men in their deceitful scheming." This is false teaching which would lead people astray and destroy the unity of the Body. In place of false teaching, Christians are to "speak the truth [of the gospel] in love" (v. 15). Such a focus allows us to "grow up into him who is the Head, that is, Christ" (v. 15).

Speaking the truth, sharing the gospel in love, means that it can no longer be used as ammunition to damn the non-Christian and shame the Christian. It is an instrument, not of destruction, but of healing. Several years ago, a student walked into my office to ask me some questions that had come up in a discussion he had had with a non-Christian friend the night before. He described not so much a discussion as a heated theological argument. He closed his description by saying, "I think I won." As a dagger of pain pierced my belly, I asked, "Is this person a Christian now?" When he replied, "No," I told him, "Then you didn't win." It was clear from his face that a new understanding of truth had just made an impact in his world. The next week, he came back to my office to tell me that his friend had given his life to Jesus.

"Speaking the truth" means so much more than speaking. In fact, the Greek word which is translated to give this phrase literally could be translated as "truthing." Many scholars have argued that the best understanding is "living out the truth."

Ephesians 4:17-32 gives examples of how and how not to live out the gospel. Paul calls his Gentile audience to "no longer live as the Gentiles do" (v. 17). Here, he hints at a metaphor that he has used earlier in the letter and which occurs throughout the New Testament. The Church has become the New Israel. Gentiles and Jews alike are now God's chosen people. Thus, Gentile Christians are no longer Gentiles who live "in the futility of their thinking" (v. 17). As such, Paul goes on to employ a form of argument common among first-century Jewish writers. He uses "vice lists" (catalogs of common Gentile actions which the Jews found detestable) to call believers away from sinful action and toward righteous behavior. Included in the list of righteous actions is a call to "put off falsehood and speak truthfully to [your] neighbor" (v. 25). So, part of "speaking [living] the truth [the gospel] in love" (v. 15) is indeed being honest with one's brothers and sisters in Christ, sometimes when it is extremely difficult to do so.

EXAMPLES TO FOLLOW

In the ancient world, writers and speakers made their points in various ways. As we do today, they could make a

logical argument or use authority to make a command.
However in that day, the best way to get a point across was
to use examples. If they wanted their audience to act righ-
teously, they might describe what righteousness was and
then demand that they act in such a manner. But the focus
of their plea would always be to point to someone who was
righteous. Paul, in his letters, identified those who were
wicked and those who were righteous (including himself and
others) and essentially said, "Act like us, not like them."

Paul ends this passage by directly pointing to the best
example, saying in 5:1-2, "Be imitators of God . . . and live a
life of love, just as Christ loved us and gave himself up for
us." God, through Christ, is the ultimate example of promoting unity in the Body.

There is, however, another example Paul uses. As he fre-
quently does, he points to himself. The NIV renders the beginning of 4:1, "As *a* prisoner for the Lord." The NRSV,
however, is more specific, as the original Greek text is, trans-
lating it, "I therefore, *the* prisoner in the Lord." In saying
that he is *the* prisoner in the Lord, Paul is not claiming that
he is the only prisoner, nor that he is the most important
one. Rather, he is indicating that in his present situation, especially as it relates to his Ephesian audience, his status as a
prisoner is his most defining characteristic. He is an example
of one who had promoted unity even to the point of imprisonment. The Ephesians are who they are in the Lord because he had proclaimed the gospel to them, the very activity
that eventually resulted in his loss of freedom. He is telling
them that if he, as "the prisoner," has no bitterness or any
other feeling that would destroy unity in the Spirit, then
they, as ones who can exercise their freedom both in Christ
and in society, have no reason to be divided. They are free to
proclaim the gospel; to speak the truth in love; and thus,
maintain the unity for which Christ died.

When I was in college in the late '70s, I had the privilege of hearing a man who had escaped from Communist

China after decades of fleeing from the Chinese Red Guard as he proclaimed the gospel of Christ. I do not remember his name or what he spoke about during the meeting, but I will never forget the conversation several of us had with him afterward. Someone asked him what his greatest impression of Christianity in America was. We were cut to the heart as he choked on his words. Tears began to form in his eyes and trickle down his cheeks. He said:

> In China, we always live in fear of the government. Many have been thrown in jail. Many have watched loved ones be killed before their eyes. We get together once a month, or every six weeks, whenever we can. We only have one Bible, so we tear it apart so that each of us can have a part to read. When we meet, we trade the Bible parts. We sing. We pray. We take Communion. We kiss one another. Then we leave. In America, you all have many Bibles in your homes *and you don't read them!* I come into an American city, and I see many churches. They argue with one another about baptism and music! You pray for the Church in China, and we are grateful. But you need to know that *we* pray for *you!*

For nearly 30 years that man, whose name I can't remember and who is probably long dead, has been for me "*the* prisoner in the Lord." Along with Paul, he has shown me that unity is not something that we can accomplish, but rather something we strive to maintain as we together proclaim and teach the gospel.

Notes:
*Ernest Best, *Ephesians* (Sheffield, England: Sheffield Academic Press, 1993), 353.

Scripture Cited: Ephesians 4:1—5:2; Philippians 1:27

About the Author: Dr. Casey is associate professor of religion at Roberts Wesleyan College, Rochester, New York.

LAWSUITS AMONG BELIEVERS

BY C. S. COWLES

From: DISCIPLE@21STCENTURY.CHURCH

To: PAUL@APOSTLES.CHRIST

Subject: Lawsuits

Dear Brother Paul,

Greetings in the majestic name of Jesus! A dispute over an inheritance has set two brothers, both on our church board, over against each other. Now they are threatening to sue each other. Both are patriarchs of large and interconnected families with vast webs of influence, and their quarrel threatens to divide the church right down the middle.

Since ours is the largest congregation in a small town, if this problem spills out into the community, it could cripple, if not destroy, our church. What can I do to head this off and, hopefully, help the two families resolve this issue?

A Concerned Believer

It seemed to be too good to be true. Yet, it was hard to dismiss the laminated checks made out to Rick, chairman of the board of trustees, paying him 10 percent interest every month on his sizeable investment. The offshore securities firm's slick brochures, featuring born-again NFL players who had major money in the company, only added to its credibility.

Rick could scarcely write contracts fast enough to keep up with those who wanted to get in on the hot deal. Savings accounts were emptied, second mortgages taken out, and retirement plans cashed in. Euphoria filled the air on "Miracle Sunday" as the congregation raised 2 million dollars for a new sanctuary, many planning to pay their pledges out of their fantastic investment earnings.

The first hint of trouble came when Rick tried to withdraw invested funds to pay subcontractors who had poured the foundation of the new sanctuary. All he got were vague references to temporary cash-flow problems. Growing desperate, he called the firm's president, only to find that the phones had been disconnected. When he discovered that the headquarters' address was a mail box service and that legal authorities were investigating, his worst fears were confirmed: He and the church had been scammed in an elaborate Ponzi scheme.[1]

Angry investors, many who lost everything, began to sue everybody in sight, including Rick and his fellow board members, who had lent their influence to the fraudulent scheme. In the wake of the disaster, Rick served time in a federal prison for selling unregistered securities; the pastor's career was ruined; businesses went bankrupt; marriages were destroyed; and the congregation dwindled to where the church had to be disorganized. Not a dime was recovered. Churches can survive financial scams and intense conflict situations, but once it boils over into the public arena of lawsuits, it is like a cancer that spreads and invades the bloodstream. As Paul put it, "You have been completely defeated already" (1 Corinthians 6:7).

When Paul describes the judicial authorities of his time as "ungodly" (v. 1) and "unbelievers" (v. 6), he was not saying that the domain of civil law and judicial process is illegitimate, but only that it is not the proper arena for the resolution of conflict among believers. To the contrary, in writing to the Romans, he states unequivocally, "Everyone must submit himself to the governing authorities, for there is no authority except that which God has established" (13:1). On more than one occasion, he availed himself of protection provided Roman citizens under the law (see Acts 16:37-40; 18:12-17; 22:15-29; 25:10-22).

Like the lone Chinese man who stood in front of a tank in Tiananmen Square, bringing the whole column to a standstill, lawsuits—and the threat of lawsuits—put the brakes on the inevitable drift of powerful institutions toward despotism. Many churches have fought court battles against discriminatory zoning laws and restrictive building codes that would severely handicap, if not eliminate, their ministries.

In that courts of law can be instruments of righteousness, why then is Paul so incensed that Corinthian believers would "dare [to] take [disputes] before the ungodly"? (1 Corinthians 6:1).

A LITIGIOUS CULTURE

As in our day when a man can press a lawsuit to stop school children from reciting the Pledge of Allegiance all the way to the Supreme Court, lawsuits had been taken to ridiculous extremes in ancient Greece. For them, court cases provided one of their chief forms of entertainment. If disputes could not be settled privately through the efforts of three arbitrators—one for the plaintiff, one for the defendant, and one acting as an impartial judge—there was a graduated system of successive courts of 40 citizens, then 200, then 400. For major cases, from 1,000 to 6,000 citizens could be impaneled on a jury. The result was that every man became a *de facto* attorney, and spent a great deal of time hearing and deciding cases. Thus, it was not surprising that converts to Christianity would bring this litigious spirit into the Church.

What was true of the Greeks is true today—only more so. In our praiseworthy passion for justice and obsession with individual rights, we have become the most litigious society in history. Attorneys outnumber physicians in many cities. There is no way to fully measure the damage done to the delicate fabric of our nation's social life by this acrimonious and adversarial spirit run amuck.

No case so appallingly illustrates both the out-of-control litigious spirit of our times and the impotence of the courts in resolving deeply personal life-and-death disputes than that which centered on Terri Schiavo, whose feeding tube was removed after 15 years in a vegetative state. The bitter feud between her husband and her family was the longest, most publicized, and most heavily litigated right-to-die dispute in United States history. Forty judges in six courts became involved, as well as Florida's state legislature, Congress, the Supreme Court, and even the president of the United States. Acrimony persists to this day.

No wonder Paul was appalled. Given his Jewish heritage, where disputes were settled quietly within the family or tribe, the whole spectacle was revolting to him. To his horror, the Corinthian church had sat on its hands while its dirty linen had been aired before a pagan court. He shames them in that a church which prided itself on its wisdom did not have anyone wise enough to judge a dispute between its members. Though lawsuits in the secular arena are routinely utilized as business strategies, they have profoundly negative consequences for believers.

THE SCANDAL OF LAWSUITS

That believers have disputes with one another is bad enough (see 1 Corinthians 1:10-12; 3:1-4). That the aggrieved may well have been "cheated" and "wronged" (6:7) is even worse. The power of Christians to seriously hurt one another is truly distressing, especially when they do it in God's name or for the supposed good of the other. "I'm doing this," said the local church leader who was circulating a petition to get me thrown out as pastor, "because I love you." *A strange way to show love,* I thought.

Such conflicts are compounded when differences become so acute, positions so hardened, and emotions so inflamed that the wounded feel they can get justice only in a court of law. Paul's response is as pointed as it is pungent.

First, *lawsuits damage the Church's witness.* There is no way to calculate how severely the avalanche of lawsuits over clergy abuse has damaged the Catholic Church in recent years and sullied its reputation. Granted, a church that has a reprehensible history of shielding immoral priests needs to be called to account. Yet, one wonders where concern for justice ends and voracious greed begins?

Second, *lawsuits are an insult to fellow believers in the Church.* Paul's reference to saints who in the messianic age will "judge the world" and "judge angels" (6:2-3) draws on a Jewish apocalyptic tradition that is largely lost to us. His point, however, is not to provide more grist for the "end times" speculation industry, but to underscore the vast difference between judges whose perspective is limited to and distorted by a world that is always already passing away and spiritually sensitized believers who view things from the standpoint of eternity. For Christians, the wisdom of "even men of little account in the church" (v. 4)—those who have the advantage of "[Christ's] power that is at work within [them]" (Ephesians 3:20)—is more to be trusted than the wisdom of the most astute "unbeliever" (v. 6; see Ephesians 2:1-3; 6:12).[2]

Third, and most devastating, *lawsuits are a denial of Christ.* Lawsuits are by definition adversarial. They are warfare by another name. They seek not reconciliation, but retribution; not resolution, but revenge; not conciliation, but condemnation. They are a reversion back to the ancient "eye for eye, and tooth for tooth" laws of vengeance specifically prohibited by our Lord (Exodus 21:24; Matthew 5:38-42).

Striking back not only compounds the injury, but locks plaintiff and defendant in a mutually self-destructive "dance of death." Conflict between two brothers who had been in business together for years escalated to the point where they decided to have it out, once and for all. They parked their cars at the end of an isolated road and walked some distance into the desert so that their shouting at each other could not be heard. Their bodies were found three days later. Apparently, one brother had beaten the other to death, but not before the vanquished brother, a very heavy man, had managed to handcuff himself to his brother's arm.

Paul, following Jesus, shows us "a more excellent way" (1 Corinthians 12:31, KJV). It is the decidedly unnatural—indeed, supernatural—way of resolving disputes through proactive self-giving and self-sacrificing *agape* love.

CULTIVATING THE FINE ART OF LOVESUITS

Instead of responding to personal loss or injury by rushing to a court of law, Paul asks rhetorically, "Why not rather be wronged? Why not rather be cheated?" (6:7). If there ever was a powerful principle on conflict resolution compressed into a tiny package, this is it: *Let it go!* That is exactly what Jesus did. "When they hurled their insults at him, he did not retaliate; when he suffered, he made no threats. Instead, he entrusted himself to him who judges justly" (1 Peter 2:23).

Peter prefaces this verse by reminding us, "To this you were called, because Christ suffered for you, leaving you *an example, that you should follow in his steps*" (v. 21, emphasis added). If we have the courage to literally follow Jesus' example of nonretaliation, we will be led through three successive stages of increasing freedom and joy.

The first is *relinquishment*. Jesus' last words on the Cross placed a mighty exclamation point at the end of a lifetime of perfect submission to the will of the Father. "Into your hands I commit my spirit." And then He "breathed his last" (Luke 23:46). In that moment, He was set absolutely free from everything and everybody who could hurt Him. As Paul says in another context, "[Christ] cannot die again; death no longer has mastery over him" (Romans 6:9). Or as E. Stanley Jones liked to say, "You can't kill a dead man. A dead man is free all over again." The author of Hebrews exults, "By his death, he [destroyed] him who holds the power of death—that is, the devil—and [set] free those who all their lives were held in slavery by their fear of death" (2:14-15).

The prayer of relinquishment means that we stop fighting for our rights, for redress of injustices, or for the punishment of our adversaries. It involves a total surrender to the will of the Father. And it is never the will of the Father that through lawsuits, or any other retaliatory means, we will be enriched at another's expense, or vindicated while another is humiliated, or triumph while another is vanquished. If we would be like Jesus, we would follow the advice of Scripture: "If your enemy is hungry, feed him; if he is thirsty, give him something to drink (Romans 12:20-21; also Proverbs 25:21).

The second stage is *reconciliation*. When Jesus prayed that unimaginable prayer from the Cross, "Father, forgive them, for they do not know what they are doing" (Luke 23:34), He reached out across the abyss and wrapped His adversaries in the warm embrace of love (see Romans 5:8, 10). In so doing, He "destroyed the barrier, the dividing wall of hostility," and created "in himself one new man out of the two, thus making peace" (Ephesians 2:14-15). In one of his poems, Edwin Markham has these lines:

> *He drew a circle that shut me out,*
> *An object of scorn, someone to flout.*
> *But love and I had the wit to win,*
> *We drew a circle that took him in.*

It was surely one of the 20th century's most dramatic moments when in the spring of 1994, Nelson Mandela, preacher of nonviolence, vaulted from prison to president of South Africa in a few short months. Even the secular press hailed the event as a miracle. A race war of unimaginable savagery had been averted.[3] It sent a further shock wave through a traumatized, yet exultant, nation when Mandela invited his white jailer to attend his inauguration as an honored guest, and gave him a seat on the dais in full view of television cameras. By that simple, but potent, gesture, he signaled to his nation—and to the world—that he sought, not redress of injustices, but reconciliation across all levels of society. His generous spirit would be emulated in a thousand ways all across his country and around the world.

The final stage is *resurrection*. After encouraging believers to let it go, Paul exults, "By his power God raised the Lord from the dead, and *he will raise us also*" (1 Corinthians 6:14, emphasis added). Death is not terminal, but transitional. It releases us from the tyranny of fixation upon past hurts, and sets us free to embrace the future with its vast horizons of new possibilities and experiences. When Paul testified, "I am crucified with Christ," that was *not* the end of the story. Nevertheless, he continued, "I live by the faith of the Son of God, who loved me, and gave himself for me" (Galatians 2:20, KJV). He lived so vibrantly, so dynamically, and so profoundly that the world has never been the same.

Rather than vengeful lawsuits, we can make the prayer attributed to Francis of Assisi our prayer:

O Lord, make me the instrument of thy peace.
Where there is hatred, let me sow love;
 Where there is injury, pardon;
 Where there is discord, union;
 Where there is doubt, faith;
 Where there is despair, hope;
 Where there is darkness, light;
 Where there is sadness, joy;

O Lord, grant that we seek
Not to be consoled but to console;
Not to be understood, but to understand;
Not to be loved, but to love.
For it is in giving that we receive,
In forgetting that we find ourselves,
In pardoning that we are pardoned,
And in dying that we are born to eternal life. Amen.

Notes:

1. A Ponzi scheme is an investment swindle in which some early investors are paid off with money put up by later ones in order to encourage more and bigger risks.

2. The Christian Legal Society and their subsidiary, Peacemaker's Ministries, have over 3,700 lawyers who donate their time to churches and parachurch organizations for the purpose of arbitrating disputes and resolving conflict.

3. Tragically, during this same month when South Africa was experiencing one of the most astonishing nonviolent revolutions in history, Rwanda, to the north, exploded in a spasm of inter-tribal genocidal violence that left over 800,000 people dead.

Scripture Cited: Exodus 21:24; Matthew 5:38-42; Luke 23:34, 46; Romans 6:9; 12:20-21; 13:1; 1 Corinthians 6:1-14; 12:31; Galatians 2:20; Ephesians 2:14-15; 3:20; Hebrews 2:14-15; 1 Peter 2:21, 23

About the Author: Dr. Cowles is the author of many books, articles, and adult Sunday School expositions. His latest book is *Who Is God? His Character Revealed in the Christ* (Beacon Hill Press of Kansas City, 2005).

8

WHO NEEDS THE RESURRECTION?

BY TERENCE PAIGE

From: DISCIPLE@21STCENTURY.CHURCH

To: PAUL@APOSTLES.CHRIST

Subject: Resurrection

Dear Brother Paul,

We know you're really into cultural adaptation for the gospel: no more circumcision, Gentiles equal to Jews, it's OK to eat bacon, etc. Well, some of us think this primitive Jewish idea of resurrection just doesn't fit the modern world of the Greeks. You need to realize that the idea of Christians getting some pathetic physical body back after they die is for us Greeks, well, just plain uneducated and unreasonable. Anyone who has been educated knows that a material body is unnecessary for the afterlife. How can a person reconcile all the messy stuff that bodies suffer with the beautiful, eternal glory of heaven? When you die, your immaterial soul leaves the material body behind for good, and what a blessing that is!

> *You have to understand that this*
> *resurrection thing is holding us back.*
> *It's laughable, and everyone knows it's*
> *unscientific. Our evangelism teams are*
> *meeting serious roadblocks over this*
> *issue, because nobody will swallow it.*
> *So we are going to go with an updated*
> *story about the afterlife—just a soul*
> *only, no resurrection. Are you as*
> *excited about this as we are?*
>
> *A Concerned Believer*

Paul first arrived in Corinth in A.D. 50, and stayed at least a year and a half, according to Luke (see Acts 18:11). He established a church that had a few Jewish converts, but was mostly made up of ex-pagans. The pagan portion of the church would have been a mixture of Roman citizens, lower-class Greeks, and foreigners. Paul was their first apostle, evangelist, spiritual adviser, and teacher. Later on, other Christian teachers would visit the church, but Paul felt a special tie and responsibility to it as its founder. After he left, he kept in touch with what was going on in the church by means of letters, visits from Corinthian Christians, or visits that Paul's coworkers made to the church.

Chapter 15 of 1 Corinthians is aimed at something the Corinthians have recently developed, which Paul believes is a major problem: some of them are denying that there is such a thing as the resurrection from the dead (v. 12). This does not mean that they doubted whether or not *Jesus* rose from the dead. In fact, part of Paul's argument in chapter 15 seems to assume that they share this belief with him. What they reject is the bodily resurrection of *Christians*. In the rest of the chapter, Paul will argue for why he believes that the doctrine of resurrection is not something Christians can give up or change. The points Paul will use in his argument with them include proofs from Jesus' own resurrection (and the consequences if it had not happened, 15:12-19), arguments from experience (15:29-32), arguments using analogies from the physical world (15:35-44), and even from prophecy (15:25-27, 54-55).

But the very first blow Paul strikes at this new false doctrine is in our target text, 15:1-11. He recites for them what we might call "the creed." It is a very brief, but very ancient, summary of the basic points of the gospel. This was, he says, the same gospel that he first brought to Corinth and that they believed in order to be saved (15:1-2).

Two main questions arise as we ponder this section and its meaning for us today: (1) Why did the Corinthians feel they needed to *change the set of Christian beliefs about the afterlife that Paul had taught them?* What was it about their culture, themselves, and the Christian doctrines that led to their taking such a radical, independent step? And (2) why does Paul begin his argument by reciting the basic gospel creed, a creed that does not even mention the resurrection of Christians in it? In answering these questions, we will see that these ancient Christian's struggle to understand their faith has some very relevant lessons for us.

SPIRIT VS. MATTER

Ancient Greek philosophers generally believed that the human *mind* was the most godly part of us and formed the "higher" part of our soul—our reason. Opposed to the reason were two contrary forces: the "animal soul" and the body. The "animal soul" represented basic instinctual drives (hunger, survival, reproduction), as well as part of our emotional life. Philosophers saw how such drives could make people do irrational and self-harming things. The other factor, the body, was a problem because it was weak, changeable, and continually demanded things of us, such as feeding. In short,

it dragged the "pure" mind down to mundane and material
things. The truly divine things were immaterial, like the
gods themselves. Hence Plato called the body the "prison of
the soul." He believed that the only way for the mind-soul to
be truly free was for it to leave the body at death and travel
up to the realm where the gods dwelled, the realm of the
stars. There the immaterial mind-soul could live, pondering
the truths which underlay the universe. He also combined
this view with a belief in reincarnation: bad or lesser souls
would be reincarnated according to what their former lives
deserved; the perfect souls of wise people would escape reincarnation and enjoy an immortal, immaterial existence.

Plato's views became very influential on later philoso-
phies, and "trickled down" to the popular level in many ways.
So, you can imagine the horror an idea like "resurrection"
would cause at Corinth—it would sound more like purgato-
ry than heaven! Why, when you had finally got rid of your
body at death, would you want another one?

Yet, the problem was greater than a clash of cultural
ideas (Greek versus Hebrew/Christian), for in Greek society,
the philosophers stood at the apex of development in education, in knowledge about the material and divine worlds.
They had contributed to mathematics, engineering, natural
history, anatomy, physics, political theory, ethics, and meta-
physics, to name just a few things. We may look back on
some of their ideas and see mistakes that look primitive and
humorous. However in the first century, the philosophers
had the same place in their society that scientists have in
ours, and philosophy commanded the same kind of respect
then as science does today when people look for explanations
of their world. So, for the Corinthians, Paul's teaching about
resurrection must have appeared not only countercultural,
but very badly ignorant. How could a material body be important for the afterlife of the soul? How could Paul foist on
them this primitive and barbaric notion of resurrection? It
just did not make sense, and so had to be corrected.

In the Greco-Roman world of the first century, other views of the dead and what happens in the afterlife existed. A widespread notion was that there is nothing at all after death. Many tombstones testify to this idea with the formula carved into them: "I was not; I was; I am not: I care not." Other inscriptions urge the readers to enjoy life all they can now, for there is only ashes and extinction afterward.

Another view of the afterlife was that there was a very murky and dim existence for the soul, sometimes in the vicinity of the grave or in Hades (as in Homer).

Then there were some who chose one of the mystery religions of the ancient world. Many of these cults promised hope for a happy afterlife on the "Island of the Blessed," if a person underwent initiation and did the proper rituals. The Corinthians must have been aware of this, for three different deities worshiped at Corinth or in the vicinity had mystery-rites associated with them (Demeter, Dionysus, and Isis). The mysteries' promise of a blessed existence was for the soul only. There was no Greek or Roman religious tradition about a resurrection for worshipers. The doctrine of bodily resurrection, therefore, probably caused problems, not only within the church, but may have seemed a problem for evangelism also, since non-Christians would certainly have found it bizarre and laughable.

STATUS-SEEKING

Recent studies of the church at Corinth have shown that there was a group of people within the church who possessed enough wealth and social status to be called middle or upper-middle class. They had houses large enough for the whole church to meet in; they held civic offices; and they could afford to carry out lawsuits in the court system (see Romans 16:23; 1 Corinthians 6:1-8). Such people sought to be upwardly mobile in Corinthian society. They were most likely to be the ones going to pagan temples with their unsaved friends and family for social reasons (see 1 Corinthians 8:1, 7-12).

That they rejected resurrection fits into this pattern of wealth and social climbing, for it would have been seen as a peculiarly Jewish idea. They decided to "fix" Paul's gospel so that it would fit in better with their society's worldview. Out with the barbaric, uneducated notion of resurrection; in with the idea of an immortal (and bodiless) soul.

THE CREED

Why does Paul quote the basic "creed" of the gospel to the Corinthians at the start of his reply to this problem? First of all, though it does not mention *believers'* resurrection, the creed does mention *Jesus'* resurrection. In fact, resurrection is such a vital part of the gospel that without it, there is no gospel at all (see 1 Corinthians 15:13-19)! And the Corinthian believers are only Christians now because they had once agreed to this creed in faith.

Foundations are very important for us. When a marriage is in trouble, a counselor will often ask the couple to reflect on what drew them together at the very start, and how they once felt about their commitment to each other. Paul is showing the Corinthians that they are not being true to their own spiritual foundations in this new teaching.

Second, he points to *evidence* for the Resurrection: There are "more than five hundred of the brothers and sisters" who have seen the risen Lord Jesus, including His original apostles, Jesus' own family members, and Paul himself (vv. 5-8). Third, Paul points to the fact that resurrection is the *faith of the church universal,* not just Paul's own idiosyncratic idea (vv. 3, 11). Since Jesus' resurrection is a divine act of God, since it is witnessed to and believed in by the Church, since it is something they once pledged themselves to, and especially because it is something that their whole saving relationship with God depends upon, the Corinthians *must* believe in resurrection. And this faith-position must take priority over any other ideas their culture would foist on them.

Immediately after this passage, Paul is going to show them what this creed must lead to: If Jesus is raised from the dead, then Christians will surely be raised also. We are joined with Him, as our Lord and our new Adam, and share His victory—not only over sin, but over death as well. It is important to note that Paul emphasizes here that Christian belief and salvation is grounded first *on what God has done through Christ by grace.* It is not merely another religious idea that some first-century people happened to have; it is about God who acted in our world.

Second, Paul emphasizes the importance of *Christian tradition.* Some scholars today are teaching that there never was such a thing as a standard or "orthodox" Christianity in the first few centuries, and that there were only competing, different visions of Jesus. But Paul is convinced here that there is an orthodox view. It goes back to the original apostles (v. 11), it was passed on to Paul (v. 3), and Paul passed it on to the Corinthians. He expected them to preserve it faithfully. Third, Paul emphasizes the authority of holy scripture, and that the Christian message fulfills it (v. 3).

PRINCIPLES

One of the most pressing issues that arises out of this passage is the question: Where is the limit of legitimate cultural adaptation of the gospel? And when does adaptation become a compromise that will weaken or destroy the core of the gospel? Which parts of culture are sinful and in need of redemption? And which parts are neutral or good? The Church cannot avoid these questions, because it is made up of people who must live within their culture.

In this case, Paul regards the creed—the most fundamental part of the gospel message about God's action on our behalf in Christ—as "supra-cultural." That means it is not subject to criticisms by, or adaptation to, the surrounding culture. It is bedrock, not wallpaper. That bedrock consists of Jesus' life, death, and resurrection; and that these things happened "for our sins," to redeem us to God; and that they happened "in accordance with the scriptures." We can also assert as equally true things that can be clearly inferred from this statement, such as that the Scriptures are inspired; that humans have sinned and need to be put right; or, as Paul argues, that believers will rise from the dead just like Jesus did (and because of Him). Because these are based on God's self-revelation in word and in deed, they cannot be changed to please social standards or conform to philosophy.

HAVE THINGS CHANGED?

In our day, there are views about death and the afterlife that are similar to many of those found in Paul's day. Some people believe there is nothing after death, and the only way the dead live on is in our memories. Some think people's spirits live on in dim fashion, helped by being remembered, or perhaps aided by some clairvoyant person. Some believe all (or nearly all) souls go someplace happy, and they automatically arrive there as if on some cosmic escalator. Some believe in reincarnation. And if we cast our eye farther afield than North America, we may encounter even stranger views.

Despite Christianity's long interaction with our culture, there are almost none outside the Church who hope specifically for a *resurrection*. Neither do people outside the Church think the deliverance of a soul depends on faith in Jesus. Often in popular movies and books, the fate of the soul is not even tied to belief in a god at all. Christianity's view of *how* one gets to heaven and *what* the afterlife is like is still as strange and distasteful to the cultural elites of today as it was in Paul's day.

And Jesus' resurrection is still controversial. For the past several Easter seasons, *TIME* Magazine and *Newsweek* have

published cover stories that revel in the most skeptical scholars' doubts about Jesus' resurrection (while they avoid acknowledging that many other scholars still believe in it). We
are still faced with the choice: conform to cultural views to
find acceptance (while betraying Scripture and the Church's
tradition), or be faithful to the teaching of Scripture, of Jesus, and the Church (while risking estrangement from our
culture). The creed of 1 Corinthians 15:1-11 reminds us that
the way for a soul to have a blessed afterlife—and what kind
of life that will be—is not dependent on our personal whim,
but on the God who created all and redeems us in Jesus.

The cultural equivalent to Greek philosophy today
would be science. Just as ancients were often in awe of philosophy, and just as philosophers served as advisers to cities
and kings in all kinds of matters, so today we respect anyone
with the label "scientist" or the claim that "science" supports
something. Think of how television commercials like to
claim "studies show . . ." and have a person in a white lab
coat tell us about their product. They are counting on people
being awed by science. The lesson for our day from 1 Corinthians 15:1-11 is that in the end, gospel trumps culture—
even the culture of science. This is not to say that science is
evil; only that it has its limitations.

Some voices in our culture may claim that "science"
proves Jesus could not have risen from the dead or that there
is no such thing as a "soul" or even that God is irrelevant to
the universe. Such people are usually not bothered by the
fact that many scientists would never make such claims. Today "science" is even being invoked to attack traditional sexual morality. The gospel, however, is based on God's self-
revelation in Jesus' life, death, and resurrection. It is beyond
criticism from created beings; it demands instead either a
"yes" or a "no" from us.

Of course, when the question is seen this way, the lesson
of this text is not just about the Resurrection. This type of
conflict faces us daily on a multitude of issues: violence, sex-

ual ethics, homosexual marriage, race relations, business ethics, the way in which politics is conducted, etc. Fill in the blank: where do *you* most feel pressure to conform to a standard that is not in harmony with the teaching and character of Jesus? And how can you live as a citizen of our culture while holding ideas that are distinctly countercultural?

Scripture Cited: 1 Corinthians 15:1-19, 25-27, 29-32, 35-44, 54-55

About the Author: Dr. Paige is professor of New Testament at Houghton College, Houghton, New York.

9

CHRISTIANS ARE HUMAN TOO

BY JOSEPH S. WANG

From: DISCIPLE@21STCENTURY.CHURCH

To: PAUL@APOSTLES.CHRIST

Subject: Suffering

Dear Brother Paul,

Rebecca (not her real name) accepted Jesus as her personal Savior when she was very young. She graduated from a Christian college. She serves the Lord faithfully in all her life. She teaches Sunday School classes, leads Bible study groups. She has led people to Christ and trained them to be good disciples of Christ.

Her husband, Joseph, is a seminary professor and serves on the board of a missionary society. About 10 years ago, while packing to accompany her husband to attend a board meeting of the missionary society, Rebecca hurt her back. She has been suffering from this since that time. This makes it very difficult for her to serve, to teach, to lead groups. Her sickness also affects her husband's ministries. From time to

> *time when her back hurts, Joseph has to*
> *cancel speaking engagement to care for*
> *her. She has seen many doctors, tried*
> *many kinds of therapy.*
>
> *Many people pray for her healing, yet*
> *she is not healed. Why does God not*
> *answer these prayers to heal her?*
>
> *A Concerned Believer*

What do you think the apostle Paul would think about Rebecca's plight? Paul himself had "a thorn in [the] flesh" (2 Corinthians 12:7). We do not know for sure what that problem was, but some scholars think it was physical frailty.

During his first missionary journey, he and Barnabas, together with Mark, went to Perga in Pamphylia. We have no details of their work there, except that John Mark returned to Jerusalem (see Acts 13:13). Perga is on the coast of the Mediterranean Sea. The weather is humid there. It is highly probable that Paul was sick and could not stay in such an environment. So, the missionary team left Perga and went to Antioch of Pisidia.

Antioch of Pisidia is located in a plateau. The weather there is much more hospitable to a sick person. In writing to the Galatians (that is, those Christians living in Antioch of Pisidia, Iconium, Lystra, and Derbe) Paul says, "As you know, it was because of an illness that I first preached the gospel to you" (Galatians 4:13). Paul also writes, "I can testify that, if you could have done so, you would have torn out your eyes and given them to me" (v. 15).

Three times Paul prayed and asked God to remove his problem, but God did not grant this request (see 2 Corinthians 12:7-9). So, he could understand firsthand what Rebecca and her husband are enduring.

SUFFERING AND CHRISTIANS

Christians have become "new creations" in Christ (2 Corinthians 5:17), but they are still human beings. They will have their share of trouble and suffering as long as they live. In addition, because they are Christians, they will have peculiar sufferings—they will suffer for the sake of Christ. In Paul's case, because he faithfully proclaimed and taught the truth God revealed to him, he was severely persecuted.

When God called Abraham, He said to him, "All peoples on earth will be blessed through you" (Genesis 12:3). Based on this in Paul's day, many believed that if the Gentiles wanted to be saved, they had to accept Jewish religion, be circumcised, and observe the Mosaic Law. By revelation, Paul claimed and taught that in Christ, God has broken the separation wall between Jews and Gentiles. The Gentiles did not have to become Jews first to receive salvation. Both Jews and Gentiles can be saved by believing in the Lord Jesus Christ. The Jews and the Judaizing Christians (the ones who insisted that Gentile Christians had to be circumcised and observe Mosaic Law) opposed Paul's teaching by attacking him and discrediting his apostolic authority. Some of Paul's opponents in Corinth accused him of arrogance, commending himself, acting from improper motives. The non-Christians opposed Paul's evangelization and persecuted him.

The apostle Paul deals at length in letters with this issue of Christians and suffering. Let's take a closer look at what he has to say in his letters to the Corinthian and Roman Christians.

FIRST RESPONSE

In 2 Corinthians 4:1-6, Paul responds to the attacks and criticisms in general terms. He claims the integrity of his character and behavior. He maintains that he did not tamper with the Word of God. The failure of many to accept the gospel is not because Paul veils the gospel, but because Satan blinds the minds and hearts of nonbelievers.

In 2 Corinthians 4:3, Paul says, "And even if our gospel is veiled, it is veiled to those who are perishing." He uses "veiled" to mean that the gospel was not accepted. This may be explained by the following consideration. In 3:12-14, Paul writes:

> Therefore, since we have such a hope, we are very bold. We are not like Moses, who would put a veil over his face to keep the Israelites from gazing at it while the ra- diance was fading away. But their minds were made dull, for to this day the same veil remains when the old covenant is read. It has not been removed, because only in Christ is it taken away.

The opponents of Paul might have claimed that it was not Moses who put a veil upon his face, but Paul, because he did not teach the full "truth" about the Old Testament—circum- cision and observance of the Mosaic Law.

IT IS NOT EASY

In 2 Corinthians 4:7-15, Paul treats the issue with greater detail. In verses 8-9, he writes, "We are hard pressed on every side, but not crushed; perplexed, but not in despair; persecuted, but not abandoned; struck down, but not de- stroyed."

The Greek word behind "perplexed" means that Paul in his conflict almost "despaired" that he could survive. In verse 10, Paul writes, "We always carry around in our body the death of Jesus, so that the life of Jesus may also be revealed in our body." He clarifies this meaning by saying, "For we who are alive are always being given over to death for Jesus' sake" (v. 11). The "always" in verses 10 and 11 indicates that Paul considers suffering not as merely occasional experience, but as the essential and continuing characteristic of apostolic service.

In this statement, "the death of Jesus" is not "died with Christ" as in Romans 6:8. The former is clarified by "we who are alive are always being given over to death for Jesus' sake" in 4:11. A similar expression occurs in 1 Corinthians 15:31, "I die every day." The meaning is that for the sake of Jesus we suffer, even to the point of death. In 4:10, "the life of Jesus" does not refer to Christians' future bodily resurrection (that is mentioned later in 4:14). "The life of Jesus" here refers to the power of Jesus' resurrection, which is manifested in the suffering for the sake of Jesus. This is clear from two other passages: "But we have this treasure in jars of clay to show that this all-surpassing power is from God and not from us" (4:7). And a similar passage dealing with suffering and the power of God from 2 Corinthians 12:9-10:

> Therefore I will boast all the more gladly about my weaknesses, so that Christ's power may rest on me. That is why, for Christ's sake, I delight in weaknesses, in insults, in hardships, in persecutions, in difficulties. For when I am weak, then I am strong.

So, in 4:7-11, death refers to suffering for the sake of Jesus, life refers to the power of Jesus' resurrection power. Suffering for the sake of Jesus gives opportunities for the power of Jesus' resurrection to manifest in the daily lives of Christians.

In 2 Corinthians 11:23-29, Paul writes about his sufferings for the sake of Christ in his missionary career.

> I have . . . been in prison more frequently, been flogged more severely, and been exposed to death again and again. Five times I received from the Jews the forty lashes minus one. Three times I was beaten with rods, once I was stoned, three times I was shipwrecked, I spent a night and a day in the open sea, I have been constantly on the move. I have been in danger from rivers, in danger from bandits, in danger from my own countrymen, in danger from Gentiles; in danger in the city, in danger in the country, in danger at sea; and in danger from false brothers. I have labored and toiled and have often gone without sleep; I have known hunger and thirst and have often gone without food; I

have been cold and naked. Besides everything else, I face daily the pressure of my concern for all the churches. Who is weak, and I do not feel weak?

If such is the case, what is the difference between Christian and non-Christian? What is the "blessing" of being a Christian? Like all human beings, Christians will suffer. Yet, suffering gives Christians opportunities to experience God's grace to sustain them. God told Paul, "My grace is sufficient for you, for my power is made perfect in weakness" (12:9). Many people know that grace is unmerited favor. However, grace is more than that. Grace is also power. In the verse just quoted, the conjunction "for" indicates clearly "grace" is closely related to "power." In fact, they are in parallel. This indicates that grace is power.

In 1 Corinthians 15:10, Paul writes, "By the grace of God I am what I am, and his grace to me was not without effect. No, I worked harder than all of them—yet not I, but the grace of God that was with me." Grace is power that makes Paul what he is. Grace empowers Paul to do what he does. When Christians suffer, God's grace, God's power, enables them to endure and overcome the suffering. Suffering gives Christians opportunities to experience God's grace, God's power.

In the opening E-mail, we talked about Rebecca who hurt her back. One day she and her husband, Joseph, went to visit a patient in a hospital. Joseph said something to comfort the patient. He told Joseph whatever he said did not mean anything, because Joseph had never suffered physically. However when Rebecca said something to the patient, he was deeply moved and encouraged. He said to Rebecca, "Because you have suffered physically, you know what you are talking about. Your words mean very much to me and encourage me greatly."

Later, Rebecca told her husband, "My physical suffering is worthwhile, because it makes me effective in ministering where you cannot minister."

COPING WITH SUFFERING

In 2 Corinthians 4:16-18, Paul talks about how to handle suffering. "Therefore we do not lose heart. Though outwardly we are wasting away, yet inwardly we are being renewed day by day." In the original Greek, Paul wrote "outer man" and "inner man." The Greeks believed that man was made up of two parts: a body and a mind (or soul) imprisoned in the physical body. However, Paul does not share this concept. Even though Paul uses these expressions, he considers a human to be a unified person. In the context of 2 Corinthians 4, the "outer man" which is wasting away is certainly to be identified with the mortal flesh that is being given up to death for Jesus' sake in verse 11. It is that aspect which is subject to the various assaults and hardships of life. Because of its vulnerability, this feature may be likened to the "jars of clay" of verse 7. Since the subjection of "flesh" to sin is not the concern here, "outer man" is not the "sinful nature" Paul discusses in Roman 7:14ff., nor the "old self" he talks about in Romans 6:6.

"Inner man" occurs three times in Paul's writings. In Romans 7:22, the "inner being" (NIV) delights in the law of God. The "inner being" of Ephesians 3:16 can be strengthened with might through God's Spirit and influences the spiritual condition and growth of the person. In 2 Corinthians 4:16, the person is "inwardly" being renewed every day. Thus, the "inner man" is that aspect which determines our intention, and is significant in influencing how we live and behave. Paul claims that even though we are wasting away by sufferings, we are renewed by Jesus' resurrection power every day. So, we do not lose heart nor become discouraged.

"For our light and momentary troubles are achieving for us an eternal glory that far outweighs them all" (v. 17). Paul compares the present suffering and the future glory. The present suffering is momentary; the future glory is eternal. The present suffering is slight; the future glory is weighty beyond comparison. Since this is true, the present suffering is bearable.

"So we fix our eyes not on what is seen, but on what is unseen. For what is seen is temporary, but what is unseen is eternal" (v. 18). If we do not want to lose heart, to be discouraged by suffering, we should intentionally set sight on, or focus attention on, the things that are unseen (eternal realities), not on the things that are seen (transient, worldly things). When suffering, people tend to pay attention to the present unpleasant experience, so Paul emphasizes the importance of intentionally focusing on the unseen eternal realities.

THE PAYOFF

Paul writes in Romans 5:3-4, "We also rejoice in our sufferings, because we know that suffering produces perseverance; perseverance, character; and character, hope." Many people ask how a person can rejoice in suffering. This is because many people think that joy is emotional exuberance. Joy can be that sometimes. However, most of the time, it is not.

Look at these examples:

- Emotional exuberance cannot be commanded, so Paul had something else in mind when he said, "Rejoice in the Lord always. I will say it again: Rejoice!" (Philippians 4:4).
- After they were mistreated by the Jewish Sanhedrin, Peter and the apostles were released. They went away "rejoicing because they had been counted worthy of suffering disgrace for the Name" (Acts 5:41).
- Paul wrote, "I rejoice in what was suffered for you, and I fill up in my flesh what is still lacking in regard to Christ's afflictions, for the sake of his body, which is the church" (Colossians 1:24).
- Jesus said, "Blessed are you when people insult you, persecute you and falsely say all kinds of evil against you because of me. Rejoice and be glad, because great

is your reward in heaven, for in the same way they
persecuted the prophets who were before you"
(Matthew 5:11-12).

These passages indicate that joy primarily is not emotional exuberance, but a sense of satisfaction derived from
some objective reality. Suffering is unpleasant. Yet, Christians will have a sense of satisfaction because suffering produces endurance, character, and hope.

Hope is powerful and can affect a person's present life
and behavior. I know a lady's story which illustrates this.
Shortly before World War II, her husband went to Southeast
Asia for a business venture. During the war, there was no
communication from him. She thought he had died, so she
did not rely on him for financial support. She worked very
hard to support herself and three children. She saved some
money for her children's education.

In order to grow the fund, she lent her money to some
companies. Around the middle of every month, she would
go to see her debtors to remind them how much interest
they had to pay her on the last day of the month. This behavior annoyed her debtors. One day she went to her debtors
to announce that they no longer had to pay the interest, nor
the principal. They were surprised, and thought she had
gone insane.

In fact, she had not. She had received a letter from her
husband, who was not dead. He had made a fortune in his
business venture, becoming a multimillionaire. In a few
weeks, he would come to take her and the children to live
with him. Compared with her newfound wealth, the money
she lent to the companies did not amount to anything. So,
she did not care to collect the debts. This hope changed her
behavior completely.

CONCLUSION

Yes, Christians are human too. We have our share of
sufferings. Yet, we are different from non-Christians. God's

grace is sufficient to sustain us in our sufferings. Moreover, the present suffering is preparing us for the future eternal glory. No wonder Christians can rejoice—even in suffering!

Scripture Cited: Genesis 12:3; Matthew 5:11-12; Acts 5:41; Romans 5:3-4; 6:6, 8; 7:14-22; 1 Corinthians 15:10, 31; 2 Corinthians 3:12-14; 4:1-18; 5:17; 11:23-24; 12:7, 9-10; Galatians 4:13, 15; Ephesians 3:16; Philippians 4:4; Colossians 1:24

About the Author: Dr. Wang is emeritus professor of New Testament at Asbury Theological Seminary in Wilmore, Kentucky.

WHEN IS JESUS COMING?

BY STEPHEN LENNOX

From: DISCIPLE@21STCENTURY.CHURCH

To: PAUL@APOSTLES.CHRIST

Subject: The Future

Dear Brother Paul:

We trust this E-mail finds you doing well in Athens. We have heard it is a magnificent city, full of temples to the gods. Are people listening to your preaching there?

There is so much we don't understand. How we wish we had been more like our brothers and sisters in nearby Berea, and listened more attentively to your teaching. Now that you are gone, we have more questions than answers, especially regarding Jesus' return. We know He will come soon, but when? And what will happen to those who have already died? Will they miss out on something? When He comes, what will happen to us, to those who persecute us, and to those who abandon the faith? Since Jesus is coming back, how are we supposed to live?

> *Should we give up our jobs or keep*
> *working? Is it really necessary for us*
> *to remain holy or have we already been*
> *registered among the faithful?*
>
> *A Concerned Believer*

Whatever other questions they addressed to Paul, the Thessalonians clearly wondered about the second coming of Jesus. Every chapter of his first letter and more than a third of his second letter refer to the *Parousia* (the technical term for the Second Coming). Perhaps the deaths—or anticipated deaths through persecution—of fellow believers heightened their uncertainty. Death naturally challenges us to think seriously about the afterlife, but these deaths raised an additional theological dilemma for the Thessalonians. Living in the earliest days of the Church and believing that Christ would return very soon, they had never faced the question of what happens to those who die before the *Parousia*. Paul, like a wise and loving father, patiently answers their questions, while raising their sights to matters eternal.

SLEEPING AND WAKING

Reference to the dead as "those who fall asleep" (1 Thessalonians 4:13) is a euphemism common to the ancient world for Jews (see 1 Kings 2:10), pagans, and Christians (see Acts 7:60; 13:36). For Christians, however, this euphemism is particularly appropriate, considering the awakening that awaits the believer who has died. By contrast, the prevailing Greco-Roman view of life after death was bleak, as expressed by the Latin poet, Gaius Valerius Catullus: "The sun can set and rise again; but once our brief light sets, there is one unending night to be slept through."[1] "Hopes are for the living; the dead are without hope," was the despairing as-

sessment of the Greek poet Theocritus.[2] Apparently, some
Christians had begun to share this hopeless perspective, as
evidenced by Paul's counsel and that of other early Christian
writers.[3]

Part of the reason for this despair among Greco-Roman
philosophers was their disbelief in a bodily resurrection. The
Athenian intellectuals listened to Paul until he spoke about
"the resurrection of the dead;" then they ridiculed him (Acts
17:32). Yet, this theological truth was nonnegotiable for the
apostle. He knew that our hope for a bodily resurrection, not
just the rising of a disembodied soul, depended on the bodily
resurrection of Jesus. This is why Paul emphasized Christ's
resurrection whenever he preached, including in person at
Thessalonica (see Acts 17:3) and later in his letters to them.
In the awkward expression, "God will bring with Jesus"
(1 Thessalonians 4:14), Paul strengthens the connection between Jesus' resurrection and ours.

When you grieve, do not do so hopelessly, Paul advised,
for those who die in Christ will also rise to live with Him.
What is more, those who die before the coming of Christ will
miss out on none of the earth-shattering events. In fact, they
will be given the position of honor among the saints. Paul is
as emphatic here as the Greek language will allow: we "will
certainly not precede those who have fallen asleep" (v. 15).

WHO SAYS SO?

Paul offers the "Lord's own word" as proof (v. 15).
Though we find no specific teaching of Jesus on this subject,
the Lord said something similar in several places:

- In Matthew 24 when He described His unexpected,
  but unmistakable, coming in the clouds to summon
  His followers (see vv. 27, 30-31, 37, 39)
- When He spoke in John 6 about raising up His fol-
  lowers on the last day (see vv. 39-40)
- When He comforted Lazarus's sister with the prom-

ise that those who believe in Him will live even
though they die (see John 11:25-26).

These verses, however, do not speak specifically about dead
believers preceding the living.

There are at least two other options. Paul could be referring to a saying of Jesus that was not written down. We
know of other such sayings. For example, "It is more blessed
to give than to receive" (Acts 20:35). And John states there
were other things Jesus did that he could have included, but
didn't (see John 21:25). Presumably, the same is true for
what Jesus said. A second possibility is that Paul is referring
to something received from Jesus through a prophetic word.
Here again, we have examples of such words from the Lord
in Acts 9:4-6, 10-16; 18:9-10; 22:18-21; 23:11; 2 Corinthians 12:9, and elsewhere in the New Testament. Whether this
was part of Jesus' teaching to His disciples that was not
recorded, or a prophetic message delivered after the ascen-
sion, Paul soothes their concern with this authoritative word
from the Lord.

HOW WILL IT HAPPEN?

Paul also provides very helpful and encouraging infor-
mation about how the end will come. Some were saying, apparently with Paul's authority, that the end had already
come, but Paul squelches that misunderstanding. Jesus will
return unexpectedly (see 1 Thessalonians 5:1-6) but unmis-
takably (see 4:16). It is unclear whether the "loud command," "voice of the archangel," and "trumpet call of God"
in 4:16 describe three separate sounds or are three ways of
describing the same sound. Perhaps the latter is the case,
since the angel's voice and trumpet are used synonymously in
Jesus' teaching in Matthew 24:31. This is one of only two
places in the New Testament that speak of archangels, the
other being Jude 9. Ancient Jewish tradition said much
more, even identifying their number as seven and naming

them.[4] The loud noise wakes the dead Christians, who then
rise to be with the Lord. After that, those who are still alive
will be "caught up together with them in the clouds to meet
the Lord in the air" (4:16).

This term "caught up"[5] has an abrupt or forceful conno-
tation, as in John 10:12 where it describes the wolf attacking
the flock, or in Acts 23:10 where the Romans forcibly snatch
Paul from the hands of the murderous mob. The latter passage is a good parallel, for that is how God will snatch His
people out of the hands of their enemies and unite them
with one another and himself. This reunion will take place in
the clouds, through which Christ ascended and from which
the angel had promised He would return (see Acts 1:9-11).

What happens next is not entirely clear. Will the Christians continue to rise to heaven, or will they return with
Christ to earth? The latter seems more likely for two reasons. First, Jesus is coming, not only to rapture His people,
but also to judge the wicked (see 2 Thessalonians 1:9-10)
and overthrow the lawless one (see 2:8). Jesus has work to do
on earth. Second, the Greek term translated "meet" usually
describes someone going out to greet another person and accompany him or her back. This is how the term is used in
Matthew 25:6 to describe the virgins who go out to meet the
bridegroom and in Acts 28:15 to describe the Roman Christians traveling more than 40 miles to meet Paul and accompany him back to Rome. One early Christian described the
scene this way:

> If he [Jesus] is about to descend, on what account
> shall we be caught up? For the sake of honor. For when
> a king drives into a city, those who are in honor go out
> to meet him; but the condemned await the judge with-
> in. And upon the coming of an affectionate father, his
> children indeed, and those who are worthy to be his
> children, are taken in a chariot, that they may see and
> kiss him; but the housekeepers who have offended him
> remain within. We are carried upon the chariot of our

Father. For he received him up in the clouds, and "we
shall be caught up in the clouds." Do you see how great
is the honor? And as he descends, we go forth to meet
him, and, what is more blessed than all, so shall we be
with him.[6]

More important than whether we return to earth or ascend
into heaven is that from that point onward, we will be with
the Lord forever.

A COMFORTING THOUGHT

What an encouragement this must have been to the
persecuted Christians in Thessalonica. One day, perhaps
soon, they would be vindicated and exalted at Christ's public
return in glory.

Paul's goal in this letter, however, was not to describe
the second coming of Jesus, but the final coming of the
kingdom of God. This puts the *Parousia* in its proper perspective. It is not just about rescuing hostages from enemy
territory, as welcome as this would be, but the final and complete invasion and conquest of enemy-held territory by its
rightful monarch. There will be no more hostages, for there
will be no more combat. When Christ returns, it means the
war is over and God has won.

Paul eagerly anticipated the kingdom of God. The unbelieving Thessalonians complained to the city rulers that
Paul was preaching "another king, one called Jesus" (Acts
17:7). In his correspondence to these believers, Paul speaks
of their having been called into God's "kingdom and glory"
(1 Thessalonians 2:12) and being "counted worthy of the
kingdom of God" for which they were suffering (2 Thessalonians 1:5). In language reminiscent of descriptions of the
Old Testament Day of the Lord, Paul pictures Christ's coming in judgment, revealed in blazing fire with His powerful
angels (see 1 Thessalonians 3:13; 2 Thessalonians 1:5-10).
The righteous will be vindicated, receiving salvation rather

than wrath (see 1 Thessalonians 5:9), and will marvel at their conquering King (see 2 Thessalonians 1:10). Those who do not know God and those who do not obey the gospel of Jesus will be punished with everlasting destruction and shut out from the Lord's presence and "majesty of his power" (2 Thessalonians 1:9). Best of all, we will experience the goal of the kingdom of God, fellowship with the King (see 1 Thessalonians 5:10; 2 Thessalonians 2:1).

Paul's words must have deeply satisfied the Thessalonian Christians. He left them in no doubt concerning the blessed state of those who have died in Christ. Death for the Christian, while sad, does not bring hopeless grief as it does to the pagans. What is more, he reminded them that Jesus may return at any moment, bringing with Him the full consummation of the kingdom of God and salvation for the righteous. Those who have already died will not only be full participants with the living, they will be given a special place of honor. In place of doubt and concern, they could now live in hope.

WHAT REALLY MATTERS?

We, too, can live in hope, if we keep in mind the blessed hope of Christ's return. Many of us have lost our grip on this essential teaching of Scripture. Instead of the watchword of the Early Church, *"Marana tha,"* meaning "our Lord, come!"[7] our watchword has become "mara not-yet," meaning "come pretty soon, Jesus." Perhaps we have become busy about our business, perhaps even busy about the Lord's business. We may have steered clear of this doctrine, fearing association with the fringe elements who interpret every event as a "sign of the times," or perhaps we have grown weary of the battles born of end-times speculation.

Our work does matter. Excesses and questions certainly exist, but Christ's return is too important to neglect. It puts our lives into perspective and allows us to live for what really matters. What venture—building a house, raising a family, fighting a war, investing dollars, or planting a field—can amount to anything unless one keeps the ultimate goal in mind? Because Jesus' return brings us to the ultimate goal—the kingdom of God—we must never lose sight of our blessed hope.

Those who maintain this hope are characterized by self-control and alertness. In Paul's words, they will "wait for [God's] Son from heaven" (1 Thessalonians 1:10). While waiting, they will "be sanctified . . . avoid sexual immorality . . . learn to control [their] own body in a way that is holy and honorable" (4:3-4). They will have "love for one another . . . lead a quiet life . . . mind [their] own business and . . . work with [their] hands" (vv. 9-11). If we are self-controlled and alert, we will remember that one day evil will be punished and righteousness rewarded, so we will choose our thoughts and actions carefully. We will remain awake and sober, armed for battle (see 5:6-8). Our ultimate goal is to please our Lord at His return. How can we be anything less than self-controlled and alert?

Because of our hope, we also experience unending joy and gratitude, knowing that with our Lord's return will come the fullness of the kingdom of God. The psalmist, anticipating the same goal, called all creation to praise:

> Let the sea resound, and everything in it,
>> the world, and all who live in it.
> Let the rivers clap their hands,
>> let the mountains sing together for joy;
> Let them sing before the LORD,
>> for he comes to judge the earth.
> He will judge the world in righteousness
>> and the peoples with equity (Psalm 98:7-9).

We cannot maintain this attitude without divine assistance. So, Paul prays that the Thessalonians will "be blameless and holy in the presence of our God and Father when our Lord Jesus comes with all his holy ones" (1 Thessalonians 3:13) and that their "whole spirit, soul and body be kept blameless at the coming of our Lord Jesus Christ" (5:23). We, too, ought to "pray continually," that is, regularly (5:17), including in those prayers fervent requests to be kept holy until Christ comes again.

Paul's counsel not only provided hope and a guideline for behavior, it also emphasized the importance of Christ's death and resurrection. When Paul wrote, "We believe that Jesus died and rose again, and so we believe that God will bring with Jesus those who have fallen asleep in him" (4:14), he was drawing a direct connection between Christ's rising from the dead and our own. Because Jesus rose from the dead, we know that He is the conquering Lord who will be "revealed from heaven in blazing fire with his heavenly angels" (2 Thessalonians 1:7). Because He conquered death on Easter morning and arose bodily, we can be assured of our own bodily resurrection when He returns. In spite of contrary winds, we must never lose our grip on the historical and bodily resurrection of Jesus for, as Paul said elsewhere, "If Christ has not been raised, your faith is futile; you are still in your sins" (1 Corinthians 15:17). "But Christ has indeed been raised from the dead, the firstfruits of those who have fallen asleep" (v. 20), therefore, "in Christ all will be made alive" (v. 22).

This is our blessed hope. *Marana tha.* Come, Lord Jesus!

Notes:

1. As cited by F. F. Bruce, *1 and 2 Thessalonians, Word Biblical Commentary,* vol. 45 (Waco, Tex.: Word Books, 1982), 96.

2. Bruce, 96.

3. The early Christian preacher, St. John Chrysostom described such Christians in his sermon on 1 Thessalonians, as cited in Peter Gorday, *Colossians, 1-2 Thessalonians, 1-2 Timothy, Titus, Philemon, Ancient Christian Commentary on Scripture,* vol. 9 (Downers Grove, Ill.: InterVarsity Press, 2000), 84.

4. They are Uriel, Raphael, Raguel, Michael, Sariel, Gabriel, and Remiel. Bruce, 100.

5. From the Latin translation of the Greek word for "caught up," we get our English word "rapture."

6. St. John Chrysostom, as cited by Gorday, 90.

7. This Aramaic phrase is found in 1 Corinthians 16:22 and the early Christian document, *Didache* 10:6.

Scripture Cited: Psalm 98:7-9; Acts 17:7, 32; 20:35; 1 Corinthians 15:17, 20, 22; 1 Thessalonians 1:10; 2:12; 3:13; 4:3-18; 5:6-8, 17, 23; 2 Thessalonians 1:5, 7, 9

About the Author: Dr. Lennox is chairperson of the Division of Religion and Philosophy at Indiana Wesleyan University, Marion, Indiana.

⑪

GROWING
IN GRACE

BY JOAN PODLEWSKI

From: DISCIPLE@21STCENTURY.CHURCH

To: PAUL@APOSTLES.CHRIST

Subject: The Thrill Is Gone

Dear Brother Paul,

When I came to Christ several years ago, there was an excitement about living for Him. Now, it seems like the Christian life is nothing more than boring routine for me. The things of the world look so enticing, and I'm having a hard time living a moral life. I must confess, sometimes I even miss the old things of my past life. Have I lost my salvation? Is there something I can do to restore the joy I felt when I first came to Christ? Help me, please!

A Concerned Believer

If the apostle Paul actually received such an E-mail, how do you suppose he would respond? Let's try to imagine his reply:

107

My dear brother or sister in Christ, thank you for sharing your deep concerns about your Christian walk. Let me assure you that what you are experiencing is a normal part of the human condition. If you are a married person, you know that the early days of your marriage were exciting. There was a sense of discovery as you and your spouse learned new things about each other. But as the days and months went by, you settled into a routine. The excitement was replaced with a sense of comfortable familiarity. Although some of the excitement had diminished, it had nothing to do with the love you had for your mate. In fact, though you were unaware of it, you were growing in your relationship. Your love for each other was deepening as you dealt faithfully with the responsibilities and challenges of each new day.

This same principle applies to when you bought your first new car or first home. There was a sense of newness and discovery. But soon you became so used to them that those things, too, lost their excitement.

The same thing happens in the Christian's life. In order to rekindle those early feelings, you must make an effort to refresh your life in Christ. I have listed here some ways to help revitalize your Christian walk.

IDENTIFY YOURSELF IN CHRIST

In my letter to the Colossians, I wrote some recommendations to help my fellow brothers and sisters in Christ find a new sense of satisfaction with their newfound freedom from legalistic doctrines. In order to gain this satisfaction, you must first have a deep appreciation and understanding of the wonderful spiritual changes that happened to you at the time of your conversion.

When Christ came into your life, you were forgiven of all your sins and promised eternal life. In addition, "you have been raised up with Christ" (Colossians 3:1). This is your new status, which requires you to live a new way of life. It seems like a difficult task, I know, but you can be assured that Christ is your power source for living the new life. He not only has set you free to live a life above moral reproach, but He has empowered you to live the true, joyful, and prayerful Christian life. I have learned that it is possible to do "all things through Christ who strengthens me" (Philippians 4:13, KJV).

To get back on track, you must "set your hearts on things above, where Christ is seated at the right hand of God" (Colossians 3:1). You must stop spending your energy and thoughts on the things that the Judaizers taught you about not handling, tasting, or touching certain things; about eating and drinking, festivals, and Sabbaths. Focus, instead, on God's character, His presence, His joy, His reality in your life. With this new focus, you will see that the former rituals and doctrines have no value. They are merely "earthly things" (v. 2).

Then you must set your mind on "things above" (v. 2). A deliberate change must pervade your whole nature, including your conduct and thoughts. You must make a decision to denounce sin and live a holy life. The material and physical things of your life should no longer have dominion over you. Rather, the sum of all your dominant desires—your will, spirit, and emotions; aims, aspirations, thoughts, and daily pursuits—need to be committed to the Lordship of Jesus Christ.

This new life is shared with the Father and Son. "For you died, and your life is now hidden with Christ in God" (v. 3). When you came to Christ, you died to the world's system, through your faith-union with Christ in His death and resurrection (see Galatians 6:14; 2 Corinthians 5:17). This new life is concealed from the unbelievers because "those who are unspiritual" (1 Corinthians 2:14, NRSV) do not accept the things of the Spirit of God.

Christ is now your life. Your key to living the risen life is to allow Christ to become the center of your universe once again. Unbelievers may not now recognize your life as hidden with Christ in God, but that will not always be the case.

When Christ comes again, "you also will be revealed with him in glory" (Colossians 3:4, NRSV).

Dedicated Christians do not live however they please. If you desire Christ to be preeminent in your life, then you will have to adopt a new set of values. This will be evident in two areas of your life: your personal holiness and your fellowship with others. With your heart fixed on God, you will avoid becoming ensnared by the world's lure and entanglements. You will see them for what they really are—purposeless, empty, and having no eternal or redeeming value. Your allegiance to Christ will monitor all of your earthly concerns and will insure that you will not lose your spiritual balance.

GIVE UP THE OLD LIFE

Be constantly aware, my brother or sister, that Christ is living through your personality and the way you live. You must consider "whatever belongs to your earthly nature: sexual immorality, impurity, lust, evil desires and greed, which is idolatry" (v. 5) as dead. These are vices that are not in keeping with the risen Christ within you. They dishonor, displease, and grieve Him (see Ephesians 4:30).

Even though you may be tempted to give in to these sins, remember that because Christ lives in you, victory over these temptations is promised as you flee from these sins. You must deprive your body of power to sin and eliminate everything in your life that is contrary to godliness by trusting Christ to give you the enabling power to do so.

There can be no holiness or maturity in a life where sin runs unchecked. These sins must be viewed like a deadly cancer that grows out of control and destroys other healthy parts. Only after the cancer has been diagnosed can treatment begin. The problems come when it goes undiscovered and untreated. Like cancer, sin carries with it its own destructive force.*

These sins of sexual perversion make God angry, and

He forbids them. "Because of these, the wrath of God is coming. You used to walk in these ways, in the life you once lived" (vv. 6-7; see also Galatians 5:19-21; Ephesians 5:6; 1 Thessalonians 4:3-6). In the process of renouncing the old nature, you need to get rid of "anger, rage, malice, slander, and filthy language from your lips. Do not lie to each other, since you have taken off your old self with its practices and have put on the new self, which is being renewed in knowledge in the image of its Creator" (vv. 8-10).

Just like the cancer that must be medically treated, radiated, or cut out, so must this old life be destroyed and the new self put under the Lordship of Jesus Christ. He has made you a new creature and is in the process of renewing your spirit daily. When you accepted Christ, you were transformed into a new life. However, with the onset of this new life, you did not receive instant spiritual maturity. That is why you are struggling, dear Christian. Growing in the grace of Christ is a lifelong process. But be encouraged, because, as Christians, "inwardly we are being renewed day by day" (2 Corinthians 4:16).

Your renewed self is the creative handiwork of God, in which it is His plan to make you like Jesus Christ (see Romans 8:29). Your new nature comes as a gift from God, not as the result of your own efforts. What you must do is to work out the salvation that God has worked in your life (see Philippians 2:12-13). One writer put it succinctly like this, "The more we are like Him, the more we shall understand Him."

As you become more like Christ, you will find it necessary to put off old patterns of thinking regarding human relationships. No longer can you discriminate against people. In Christ, "there is no Greek or Jew, circumcised or uncircumcised, barbarian, Scythian, slave or free" (Colossians 3:11).

In my first-century world, racial, religious, cultural, and social barriers separating people were deep-seated and formidable. Jewish people refused to enter a Gentile house. They would not eat a meal cooked by Gentiles, nor buy meat

prepared by Gentile butchers. There were cultural distinc-
tions between the barbarians and the Scythians, though both
were particularly brutish and savage people. The cultured,
educated Greek or Jew, even after having believed the
gospel, still looked with contempt upon them. They failed to
recognize that the gospel breaks down walls. It does not
classify people by race, tribe, nationality, or class, "but Christ
is all, and is in all" (v. 11).

Now that you understand why you must kill off all these
ways and attitudes which are displeasing to God, you must
replace them with qualities that characterize the life of Jesus
within you.

PUT ON THE NEW IDENTITY IN CHRIST

"As God's chosen people, holy and dearly loved, clothe
yourselves with compassion, kindness, humility, gentleness
and patience. Bear with each other and forgive whatever
grievances you may have against one another. Forgive as the
Lord forgave you" (vv. 12-13). These qualities are necessary
to fostering healthy church and community relations. Compassion is vital because, with it, we demonstrate a heart for
the hurting and burdened and respond to their hurts and
sorrows. Kindness is exhibited when we are as concerned
about our neighbor's good as about our own. Humility
means we serve others without caring whether it is noticed
or not. Gentleness does not condemn, but makes us willing
to make allowances for others. Patience refrains from exact-
ing revenge against enemies and is willing to endure wrongs.

These virtues lead to forbearing and forgiving. By bearing with and bearing up your brother or sister who sins, you
demonstrate love and obedience to the law of Christ. In other words, you must model a forgiving spirit, as exemplified
by Christ himself on the Cross when He said, "Father, forgive them" (Luke 23:34).

"And over all these virtues put on love, which binds

them all together in perfect unity" (Colossians 3:14). Dear Christian, you must realize that those who are loved by God are to be loving of others. This is the most important quality in your life. Love is the very glue that produces unity in the Church. Your love for God will be proved by the way you love others in Christ Jesus.

ORDER YOUR PRIORITIES IN CHRIST

Friend, is there anything in your life that dishonors Christ? Is it well with your soul? Does the peace of Christ rule in your heart at any given moment, regardless of issues? Then "let the peace of Christ rule in your hearts, since as members of one body you were called to peace" (v. 15). When the peace of Christ abides in your heart, you will live in unity and harmony with others.

Maintaining peace requires a grateful spirit (see Colossians 2:7; 4:2). Gratitude will come naturally when you reflect and respond to all God has done for you.

In order to prevent falling back into your old ways, you must schedule time to read and study God's Word regularly. The truths of Scripture should permeate every aspect of your life and govern every thought, word, and deed. "Let the word of Christ dwell in you richly" (v. 16). Relate every issue to the Word to determine whether it pleases or displeases the Lord. Look for clear principles or statements in Scripture that can be applied to the particular matter at hand.

When the Word of God dwells richly within you, you will want to sing with gratitude to God. As you worship with others together in the Body of Christ, the beautiful music of the church will express externally your internal emotion of gratitude. You will be expressing your thankfulness with your heart as well as your lips. Your soul will be uplifted as you "sing to him a new song" (Psalm 33:3).

From this heart of gratitude will come the desire to live entirely for Christ. "Whatever you do, whether in word or deed, do it all in the name of the Lord Jesus, giving thanks to God the Father through him" (Colossians 3:17). If you are cleaning, shopping, exercising, preaching, eating, driving your car, mowing the lawn, or working at your job, it is all to be done in the name of the Lord Jesus.

So my dear Christian friend, I trust that this answers your questions. I have presented the norm for the Christian life. It is a life that is lived without reluctance or legalistic duty, but with thanksgiving (see 1 Corinthians 10:31). To put on this new lifestyle is to put on Christ. Your life goal should be Christlikeness.

As with everything in the Christian life, growing in Christlikeness cannot occur through your own power. You must allow God to mold and make you by the power of Christ that lives within you. In natural growth, sometimes the process is slow, sometimes it comes in spurts. So it is with spiritual growth. Be patient! Christ will cause His life within you to flourish and bring glory to the Father because that is His will for you.

Notes:

*David E. Garland, *The NIV Application Commentary, Colossians/Philemon* (Grand Rapids: Zondervan Publishing House, 1998), 217.

Scriptures Cited: Psalm 33:3; Luke 23:34; 1 Corinthians 12:14; 2 Corinthians 4:16; Philippians 4:13; Colossians 3:1-17

About the Author: Rev. Podlewski is an ordained minister in The Wesleyan Church. Semi-retired, she is doing interim pastoring and writing adult Sunday School curriculum.

12

CONTENTED CHRISTIANS

BY ALEX VARUGHESE

From: DISCIPLE@21STCENTURY.CHURCH

To: PAUL@APOSTLES.CHRIST

Subject: Discontentment in the Church

Dear Brother Paul:

Recently I was reading the first letter that you sent to Timothy a long time ago. It became apparent to me that you were extremely concerned about the infiltration of the Church by false teachers who were corrupting Christians with their ideas. You may be saddened to hear that this problem has never left the Church, and nearly 2,000 years later, it continues to be a source of heartache for the faithful.

In recent years there has been a significant increase in the number of those who have been exploiting the gospel to increase their wealth and prosperity. Masses of people turn to these so-called preachers, thinking that they present ideas that are true to the Christian gospel. Many are confused about what it means to be an authentic Christian.

How would a Christian know that a person is presenting ideas that are not distinctly Christian? What should be the priorities of a Christian? Can a person be Christian and at the same time wealthy? In a world that seems to associate contentment with wealth, how can a Christian find true contentment?

A Concerned Believer

As we did in the previous chapter, let's imagine that Paul himself answered the above E-mail. Here is what he might have to say:

Dear 21st-century Christian disciple, grace and peace. I am glad to hear that nearly 2,000 years later, people are reading that letter that I sent to my spiritual son Timothy.

As you have imagined, I am saddened to hear about the continued exploitation of the gospel by those who seek wealth and prosperity in the name of Jesus Christ. I have heard that technological developments in your time have helped these false preachers to bring the gospel of health, wealth, and prosperity into the living rooms of their unsuspecting victims. Well, in my time also there were plenty of these preachers who went from town to town to sell their message. These wandering preachers were all too common in both the Christian world and the non-Christian world. They were able to attract large crowds of people who loved to hear them talk about philosophical ideas, and make arguments with their clever ideas. Sadly, a whole city would turn out to hear these teachers of philosophy. The Greek people loved anyone who could speak with powerful and eloquent words.

Even in my time, a person could make a fortune with the power of eloquence and oratorical skill. And sadly, these types of false teachers found the churches in my day as a place to promote themselves and their false religious ideas, and to increase their wealth and fortune.

DISTINCTLY CHRISTIAN

You asked me how would a Christian know that a person is presenting ideas that are not distinctly Christian? As I mentioned in my letter to Timothy, one should ask if such teaching agrees with the sound teaching of Jesus Christ, and if such teaching demonstrates true godliness. True Christian faith proclaims what was taught and lived out by our Lord. As you know, Jesus came to preach the good news of salvation to all humanity. He did not come to seek fame and glory, wealth and power, or status and recognition by others. There was nothing unreal about Him or His teaching. He lived among the poor, gave them comfort and hope, and even gave His life to save the sinful world. To Him, those who were happy and content were the poor in spirit, those who mourn, the meek, those who hunger and thirst for righteousness, the merciful, the pure in heart, the peacemakers, and those who were persecuted for the sake of righteousness. He was humble, not conceited or proud. He did not enter into argument and debate with others on controversial issues, although He had to face plenty of opposition to His teaching. He did not cause strife or division among people with baseless arguments. He exemplified godliness in life through His humility before others and obedience to God.

Just as you have in your day, there were many false teachers in my day also who did not follow the example of Jesus. These false teachers, though they did not know the truth, were conceited and interested only in promoting themselves and their unfounded ideas. They were puffed up and arrogant. They thought that their arguments with others or wordy speeches were necessary to win others to the Christian faith. They did not like those who challenged their ideas, and would not have hesitated to attack their character with slanderous words. These preachers' words only promoted envy and dissension. Their arguments did not edify others, but often ended in debates and confrontations.

They practiced a commercialized form of Christianity, which they sold to those who ignorantly followed them. They showed piety before others simply for the sake of enlarging their wealth. Those who followed them were people who did not know the truth and were distorted in their thinking. True godliness was not the source of their contentment, but rather they thought the money made through false religious teaching would make them content.

Sadly, these kinds of false teachers still continue to prey upon people. I urge you not to be entrapped by these false teachers, but to follow values and principles that exemplify the life and teachings of our Lord Jesus Christ. This way of life will spare you from many of the heartaches resulting from following non-Christian values and principles.

CHRISTIAN PRIORITIES

You have asked about priorities in Christian life. Now, let me suggest some things that should top the list of priorities for a true Christian disciple:

Godly living with contentment. This means one's devotion to God and determination to be detached from all material things with which others seek to bring happiness to their lives.

Keep a proper perspective on wealth. Wealth and money should never become an obsession to a Christian disciple. We did not bring wealth into the world; certainly we will not take wealth with us when we leave here. Money has the power to corrupt people. It can become a snare to one's life, an entrapment that chokes all happiness out of a person. The craving for money will compel people to do senseless things, including the forsaking of faith in Christ.

Live and be content with very few material resources. Even those who possess much wealth in life should be content with basic necessities, such as food, clothing, and shelter.

Aim to possess righteousness, godliness, faith, love, steadfastness, and gentleness—qualities that are enduring and uniquely Christian. Righteousness is one's right conduct and rightness in relationship with God and others. Those who seek the path of righteousness avoid wrongful actions or actions that harm others.

Godliness of life is one's piety, reverence for God and humility before others. Some people are good at showing their piety through external performances, like the Pharisees among whom I lived before my conversion to Christian faith. Christian godliness is an inner quality, a quality that shapes and guides a person's life.

Faith is one's trust in the trustworthiness of God. Those who have faith respond to the grace of God at work in their lives with their utter loyalty to Him. Those who have faith respond positively to what God is doing in their lives, and their lives show evidence of their faith through their good works.

The quality of love is something we learn from the example of Christ. Love is not just an emotional response, but a commitment to give one's life for the sake of others. Love has, thus, a sacrificial element; it is emptying out oneself for others. This is the kind of love that God has for sinful humanity. Only those who have experienced God's love for them are able to love others as God loves them.

Steadfastness is one's decision to stand firm in the Christian faith and commitment to Christ regardless of the adversities of life. It is "hanging in there" with courage and patience, faith and endurance, and hope in the victory that lies ahead.

Gentleness is more than soft-mannered ways of life, or

soft-heartedness. It manifests in forgiveness when others offend, in humility before God and others, and in right treatment of others. A truly gentle person is also firm in opposing any unrighteousness, any wrong done against others.

A true Christian must remain in unswerving loyalty to the confession of Christian faith. I wrote my letter to Timothy when keeping faith was difficult because of intense opposition from the enemies of the gospel. Only by faith could one have fought the battle to remain loyal to the confession of Jesus as Lord, made when a person was baptized into the Christian faith before many witnesses. Jesus, when He stood before Pilate, did not waver, but gave an affirmative answer when He was asked, "Are you the king of the Jews?"

Christians who are rich should set their hopes in God and not on their wealth. They should recognize that their wealth comes from God. God gives them wealth to be generous in doing good deeds to others. Certainly, God will reward them with true life, which they cannot gain with their wealth.

Now to the question, "Can a person be Christian and at the same time wealthy?" Certainly, there were Christians who were rich in the first century. Since God is the giver of all good things, we should not think that wealth is evil or bad. We should not think that a wealthy person cannot be a good Christian. Wealth itself is not bad, and wealth should not be regarded as a hindrance to one's faith. Of course, if one does not take care to place wealth in the lowest priorities of life, it can become a hindrance to faith. The source of evil is one's *love* of money, not money itself.

TRUE CONTENTMENT

In a world that seems to associate contentment with wealth, all Christians, both rich and poor, should ask themselves, "How can a Christian find true contentment?" There is nothing particularly virtuous about being poor. Poverty is not a sign of committed Christian faith. Indeed, poverty can lead people to live a discontented life. The poor should not think that gaining wealth will bring contentment to their lives. As I have written to the Philippians, "I have learned to be content whatever the circumstances" (4:11). Happiness that one seeks through wealth cannot last, but happiness that comes through one's love for God and love for the neighbor will endure through all difficulties of life.

Be content in your godliness. The grace of the Lord Jesus Christ be with you.

PRINCIPLES FOR CHRISTIAN LIFE

In light of the response Paul might have written to our imagined E-mail, this portion of Paul's letter to Timothy (6:3-19) invites Christians today to reflect on the following principles for Christian life:

1. Genuine preaching and teaching of the gospel aim to promote godliness in life. Therefore, it is imperative that Christians avoid the teaching of those who have made the Christian faith a commodity for sale. Just as in the days of Paul, we see a flurry of the activities of those who market Christianity through TV and other media. Christians should have the discernment of the truth of the gospel, so that they can easily identify those who are peddlers of the gospel. The commercialized Christian faith sells health, wealth, and prosperity. Many who preach this form of Christianity are practicing a career. On the other hand, for genuine preachers of the gospel, preaching is a calling from God, a vocation to which they have committed their lives.

2. Authentic Christians do not cause dissensions and divisions or claim to have a corner on the truth or slander those who disagree with them. The spirit of Jesus Christ is a spirit of humility before those who may disagree with us or be different from us.

3. Contentment that comes through godliness is that which Christians should seek. True contentment is sufficien-

cy that comes from one's commitment to live a godly life. It is sufficiency that is found in one's relationship with Christ.

4. Wealth cannot bring contentment to life. Those who are preoccupied with wealth will only add sorrow to their lives, because they are never content with the wealth they have. The more they have, the more they want to make; and the thirst for wealth does not go away. The end result is an unhappy and discontented life. One's unbridled desire for money will only lead to actions that are evil and hurtful to others.

5. We should not seek more than basic necessities of life. Christians should not buy into the world's "bigger is better" philosophy. Contentment that one seeks through extravagant life is short-lived because there is always the never-ending appeal for the latest product in the market or the fastest car or a more luxurious house or fancier clothing.

6. The qualities of righteousness, godliness, faith, love, steadfastness, and gentleness should define and shape the Christian's life. These are qualities that our world does not promote. In a morally bankrupt world in which we live, these qualities of life are the best witness of our commitment to live as authentic disciples of Jesus Christ.

7. Commitment to the faith we confess should be evident in all spheres of our life, not only in our church and home, but in the market places of our existence. Christians, when they confess Jesus as Lord, are taking a firm stand with Christ, and for Christ in our world which desperately needs to experience Christ.

8. Wealth should not distract us from our commitment to follow Christ. The wealthy should not think that they can buy eternal life with their wealth. Wealth without a generous heart means an impoverished soul without any hope of eternal life. Those who claim their heritage to the theology of John Wesley should reflect on his words, "Earn all you can, save all you can, give all you can."

SUMMARY

Finally, here in a "nutshell" are ways for Christians to be content:

A disciple of Jesus Christ should not teach or promote or support doctrines that are contrary to the teachings of Jesus Christ.

A disciple of Jesus Christ should not make money or accumulate wealth through practices that are contrary to the teachings of Jesus Christ.

A disciple of Jesus Christ should seek contentment through godly living.

A disciple of Jesus Christ should be a faithful witness of Jesus Christ in the world.

Scripture Cited: Philippians 4:11; 1 Timothy 6:3-19

About the Author: Dr. Varughese is professor of religion at Mount Vernon Nazarene University, Mount Vernon, Ohio.

13

CHRISTIANS SHOULD NOT GIVE UP

BY MARK A. HOLMES

From: DISCIPLE@21STCENTURY.CHURCH

To: PAUL@APOSTLES.CHRIST

Subject: Falling Away from the Faith

Dear Brother Paul,

You probably already know that a few of our missionaries have been thrown into prison for preaching about Jesus Christ. Some of the people in our small group are afraid. We have been hearing reports of Christians being persecuted in this country for their faith. I have tried to persuade the group that the rumors are probably exaggerated, but they are convinced we are next. What will we do if it should happen to us?

All of this has taken its toll, and our group is becoming smaller. What should I do? What can I tell these people to encourage them in their commitment to the faith?

A Concerned Believer

Paul was in prison! Not that this was unheard of. Bad things happen. He had been incarcerated a number of times as he traveled in his ministry. Nor was a Christian being arrested an unusual event during the persecution by Nero, the Roman emperor who reigned during this time. But despite Paul's past experience of imprisonment, his present incarceration in Rome seems to have raised a level of concern for Paul's well-being, and the impact this event was having on the followers of Christ. In an endearing letter to Timothy, his "dear son" in the faith (2 Timothy 1:2), Paul shares insights into his experience and how Timothy and others like ourselves should respond to this and other challenges to our faith.

First, Paul's present circumstances were different than the house arrest he had experienced earlier in Rome, when he had appealed to Caesar in the face of trumped-up charges made by the Jewish leaders in Jerusalem. This time he was housed in a cold Roman cell, bound by chains (see 1:16; 2:9).

Second, the possibility of Paul being executed was quite real (see 4:6-8). Even though he had faced persecution and death a number of times during his travels—stoned and left for dead, beaten, shipwrecked, bitten by a poisonous snake, etc.—his words carry a sense of finality. He was being "poured out" (v. 6) like an offering before God. The ultimate expression of commitment was imminent. Yet, he articulated a peace about the whole idea. Paul was accepting the possibility of his death with the comfort that he had led a faithful life, for which he anticipated an eternal reward.

What appears to be most challenging to Paul is the fact he was abandoned by many of his followers. He tells Timothy that He had been left to fend for himself during his first appearance in court (see v. 16), and was now apparently alone, except for Luke (see v. 11). In what was probably an overstatement, he declares that everyone in the province of Asia had abandoned him, including two named Phygelus and Hermogenes (see 1:15). Others, like Hymenaeus and

Philetus, had begun to teach false beliefs that were misleading people in the faith (see 2:17-18). Another follower named Demas had gone back to the world (see 4:10).

Paul had sent the few remaining workers to other towns and regions. One ray of sunshine had come from a man named Onesiphorus who had made a point to search for Paul in Rome, unashamed of his imprisoned state (see 1:16-17). Now virtually alone, Paul laments the damage inflicted upon him by Alexander the metal worker (see 4:14) and desires Timothy to come quickly, and to bring Mark (see v. 9).

This exodus by Paul's people reveals the reality of life's impact on the faith. By his own explanation, some had left the faith because of the lure of the world; others because they no longer believed the teachings of Christ, choosing to proclaim an errant message. Still, the tone of Paul's letter implies that there were other influences having their effects upon the church. Two possibilities are apparent: (1) Paul's imprisonment had become an embarrassment to some, causing them to distance themselves from the apostle and the faith. (2) Nero's aggressive persecution of Christians was taking its toll. Those not wanting to suffer for the faith were retreating to the safety of paganism.

Though he does not accuse Timothy of any of these reactions, Paul's letter addresses them as though he were unsure how Timothy might react to the news of his imprisonment. Maybe his protégé would be embarrassed or frightened as well. In explaining his circumstances, Paul argues for the propriety of his ministry, stating his service was in keeping with those of his forefathers, which he has performed with a clear conscience (see 1:3). He blames his imprisonment on his faithfulness to his God-given task (see vv. 11-12). He challenges Timothy, "Do not be ashamed to testify about our Lord, or ashamed of me His prisoner. But join with me in suffering for the gospel, by the power of God" (v. 8). Was Timothy having second thoughts about the faith, or was Paul just exercising an ounce of prevention? Whatever the motives for his writing, the advice he shares with Timothy remains helpful even today as circumstances challenge our commitment to follow Jesus.

SCANDALS EVERYWHERE

There is nothing like a scandal or persecution to bring about major destruction to God's church. Sadly, we can recall too many occasions when pastors and prominent leaders of the Church have failed morally, bringing disgrace and doubt before the public. As a result, some followers have become disenchanted with the faith, believing if these fallen leaders were examples of the Church as a whole, it is better not to be involved. Others back away because of the ridicule and questions these situations cause among friends and associates. It simply becomes less embarrassing around the water cooler at work if one is not identified as a Christian and stereotyped as one of the fallen.

A fellow pastor underwent an uncomfortable experience in a local fast-food restaurant when a group of people sitting at a table close by began to malign him, denouncing him for a number of abuses commonly reported in the media concerning the improper behavior of certain ministers. Though this man was not guilty of any of the improprieties exercised by others, he was condemned by association. He admitted the experience was both embarrassing and hurtful. Fortunately, he was able to handle the situation with grace, and continues on in his ministry.

It does not require a failure by a leader or persecution for people to entertain second thoughts about following Jesus. Often defections come from the daily challenge of temptations or a clash of wills with God or the local congregation. Sometimes it happens when close friends, previously committed to God, fall away, or just by being confronted by our own moral limitations. Any number of life's experiences can leave us feeling threatened, frustrated, or defeated, making the possibility of giving up the faith an attractive option. Whether the cause is international or local, public or private, every Christian at some point in life finds his or her commitment to God challenged. What should we do when the inevitable occurs? Paul's letter to Timothy contains a wealth of advice for us.

LOOK WITHIN

Paul's first directive challenges Timothy to look within himself. This is a great place to direct our attention when life is challenged from the outside. It helps us to gain perspective by seeing the issues with greater breadth than if we merely fixate upon those external issues. There are three inner foundations that Paul knew would support Timothy: his inherited faith, his spiritual gift, and the presence of the Holy Spirit.

In the darker times of doubt or conflict, it is easy to feel alone or abandoned. This feeling has a strong negative influence upon a person, resulting in the desire to give in. After all, what can one person do when everyone else has given up and walked away? By looking within to our heritage, we discover, despite how we might feel, that we are not alone. Nestled deep within is a heritage of witnesses who still stand beside us, even though they may no longer physically exist. All of us have people who have strongly influenced our lives for the faith that enable us to find inspiration to continue; people who have withstood similar experiences yet remained faithful; people who stood alongside us in the past, whose influence will not abandon us in the present.

For Timothy, it was his grandmother and mother. Both had contributed to a legacy of faith that was now entrusted to him. These ladies underwent challenges to their faith, and stood their ground. As it had been possible for them, it would be possible for Timothy. Thus, Paul challenged him to continue in the faith that he was taught as a defense against false teachings by which many were being deceived (see 3:13-15).

The same is true today. Whether biological or relational, we all stand where we are in the faith upon the shoulders of those who have withstood the challenges of this world before, and have persevered. When it seems as though we are alone, we must look within for the heritage that enables us to stand even when we feel weak.

Early in my Christian experience, one of my uncles through marriage had been going through some deep trials in his life. Lesser Christians would have given up, possibly blaming God for their predicament. However, one day when we were together, I heard this suffering saint begin his prayer, "O God, You have been so good to me." The words went straight to my heart and have lodged there ever since. I hope I never find myself tested by the circumstances this godly man was facing at the time. Still, I have found that on those occasions when I have been challenged, these words come back to me and, with them, the resolve to press on. If hardship or disappointment is making you feel alone, look within for the fellowship of saints that enables you to continue.

Paul's second internal challenge to Timothy deals with his spiritual gift. No other writer within the Bible gives us such a wealth of understanding on this topic as Paul (See 1 Corinthians 12—14; Ephesians 4:7-13). His teaching, simply stated, is that God gives to each of His followers a means of grace by which we can participate in ministry to the Church and world. The potential of these gifts is unlimited, as they enable us to do what we otherwise could not. God expects that once we receive these supernatural abilities, we will be faithful in exercising them.

In times of challenge, one of our first inclinations is to disconnect until the heat is over. Yet as we do, we lose our incentive and purpose within the faith. There is something about ministry that helps us keep our perspective and commitment. Thus, Paul tells Timothy, "Fan the flame" (1:6). The word-picture is insightful. We have all coaxed a dying fire back to flame by blowing on or fanning its embers. Paul challenges us to call our God-given gifts forward so that our participation will be renewed. This is done through involvement and usage. As we find ourselves active within ministry, we become steadily dependent upon God's provisions for our service. Thus, our gifts are brought to their full expression.

In construction, whenever an arch is structurally weakened, it is made stronger by placing more weight upon it, causing the principles by which it naturally works to come into play. The same is true for humankind when we are challenged in life. Despite our desire to come out from under the pressure, the best place for us to be is under the influence of our daily ministries for which we have been gifted. Remaining faithful to these causes our dependence upon God to grow, and His gifts to strengthen us.

The third area Timothy is to consider within is the presence of the Holy Spirit. It is a reminder for Timothy not to fall into the trap of self-reliance. When our foundations begin to crumble and our world comes apart, we are quick to assume the ability for restoration lies within ourselves. We attempt to face our challenges by our own strength, which only sets us up for certain failure. We become easy prey for the evil one. The Spirit enables us to withstand life's challenges by so many means, yet Paul shares only three: "power," "love," and "self-discipline" (1:7). Expressed in other words, we could say "ability, motive, and control." All of these are essential for our continued commitment to the faith and service to God.

The ability to stand in the face of challenge and doubt comes from the indwelling influence of the Spirit, whom Jesus said gives us power when He is received (see Acts 1:8). Jesus knew this would be essential to enable His disciples to fulfill and withstand the tasks and challenges they would face in building God's kingdom in this world. If it was true for the disciples, can we stand by any other means?

Challenges to our faith quickly reveal the motives we

exercise. Like silver refined in fire, everything that is not genuine quickly burns away. If our motive is not pure, we find ourselves devoid of reason and purpose and our commitment crumbles. Of the many possible motives we can have for following Jesus, only one can withstand the fires of trial and challenge—love. It is the love that is brought into us by the presence of the Holy Spirit, making our life with God pure and genuine. If our reason for serving God is love, no matter how hot the fire becomes, our motive will only be made more pure and complete. Lesser foundations to commitment simply burn away and leave us crumbled.

When challenged, how much control do we maintain? Panic, fear, anger, shame, any number of emotions well up within us. If allowed, they can assume control of what we do and think. There is nothing like a problem in life to elicit knee-jerk reactions based more on emotion than appropriate judgment. The Holy Spirit can enable us to brush aside the superficiality of emotion to find the kernel of truth within the issue, allowing us to maintain perspective and control. If led by the Holy Spirit, we can withstand the lesser influences that seek for control.

SEEK GODLY CONTENTMENT

We live in a society of seemingly limitless options. As a result, we are not only given numerous choices, but also ample means to avoid unpleasant or challenging situations. We can shop for whatever best fits our interests or desires. This influence is even felt within today's church, as people pick and choose the congregation that best relates to them and their perceived needs. In some ways, this is good, as it allows for growth and development. But in other ways, it is destructive, because it allows us to avoid challenges regarding our faith and person. If something becomes too uncomfortable, we simply find another fellowship. We may feel more comfortable, but the areas that need to be changed go unaddressed. Overall, we are becoming a society that is adept at avoiding confrontation and hardship, leaving this vital area of the faith sorely undeveloped.

In Philippians 4:12, Paul makes a statement that sounds foreign to us. "I have learned the secret of being content in any and every situation." We usually equate contentment with positive circumstances. Paul's dictum is all-inclusive. What a statement of holiness! It speaks of the ability to accept the difficulties of life with a willingness to live within and above them by the grace of God. Yet, this is not a statement of personal ability. Paul concludes by writing, "I can do everything through him who gives me strength" (v. 13). If we are to experience holiness during this lifetime, it will require the desire of the first statement by the means of the second. In place of fleeing the negative, uncomfortable, or scary, we resolve to live within the circumstance, fully trusting that God will provide the means by which we meet each challenge with a faithful, consistent witness and lifestyle. Paul could live this expression while enduring the harsh conditions of lonely imprisonment, anticipating his own demise. Timothy could embrace this as he faced a world given over to persecution, false teachings, and desertions.

Adversity is a natural part of living. What we do with it will determine its influence upon our life and our eventual character. Some feel that avoidance is the best response, where confrontation and endurance actually will lead us into a life of contentment, despite the circumstance, and a committed faith that enables us to trust in God, enabled to do everything in which we are challenged. Paul Tillich once wrote that people so inclined in their faith and commitment to God can look at every circumstance with the belief, "never-the-less God!" Or as Paul could write to Timothy, "That is why I am suffering as I am. Yet I am not ashamed, because I know whom I have believed, and am convinced that He is able to guard what I have entrusted to Him for that day" (2 Timothy 1:12).

Scripture Cited: Philippians 4:12-13; 2 Timothy 1:2-18

About the Author: Rev. Holmes pastors The Wesleyan Church in Superior, Wisconsin.